Using her story and the stories of others, Linda invites the reader into a conversation about life's inevitable and unfair hurts. Her in-depth knowledge of Scripture and engaging writing style help the reader courageously embrace trials, persevere through suffering, and use hurts as a means of going deeper with God. Linda's book and Bible study are sure to give hope and courage to everyone, no matter where one may be in life's unpredictable journey.

—Laura Magnin McDonald, MA, LPC, co-founder of Christian Insight for Life, author of *The Heart Handbook, How You Think...Determines the Course of Your Life* and *Christian Insight for Life: A Devotional*

It is a great honor to endorse this book, *Healing Hurts*. I've watched firsthand as Linda brings hope and encouragement to women and men alike through the years. She speaks openly from her own pain and healing. It will strengthen your faith, while urging you onward in growing closer to the heart of God and truly trusting Him with whatever happens next. I believe you will be encouraged and find new hope by the words that are written in the pages of this book.

—Donna Peters, Pastor, Groups & Connections, Northplace Church

It is my honor and privilege to endorse Linda Kennedy's latest book. Linda and her husband, Gary, have experienced life like very few people have. They have come out victorious, even though life has dealt them some tough hands. Her encouragement in this book will lift your hearts and give you hope for whatever you have faced or will face in the future. She is an inspiration to all of us who have known her and Gary!

—Rusty Westerfield, Pastor

Linda Kennedy's book "Healing Hurts" is a must-read book for anyone who is suffering, or has suffered and is questioning God. Her real-life experience is an incredible testimony of how to survive great suffering through faith in God and understanding His promises. She provides real examples and stories of others who have suffered greatly and shows how God uses those experiences for His glory. He can take our ashes and make something beautiful. Linda's book can help one see that God cannot only get you through the hurt and suffering, but He can use it to mold and shape a person who keeps their eyes on Him through it all. This book can help anyone who is suffering to see that God is still with them, for His love is greater and deeper than any suffering we can experience.

—Dr. Magdalena Battles, Author & Conference Speaker

healing
hurts

Linda Kennedy

HEALING HURTS

Linda Kennedy

INTELLIGENT DESIGN PRESS

HEALING HURTS by Linda Kennedy

ISBNs   978-1-953625-03-8 (Paperback)
        978-1-953625-04-5 (eBook)

Copyright © 2021 Linda Kennedy.

Cover photo by Karolina Grabowska.
Cover and book design by Kelley Creative.

Published by Intelligent Design Press, an imprint of Kelley Creative.

Unless otherwise indicated, all Scripture quotations are taken from
the Holy Bible, New Living Translation, copyright © 1996, 2004, 2007
by Tyndale House Foundation. Used by permission of Tyndale House
Publishers, Inc., Carol Stream, Illinois 60188. All rights reserved.

Scripture quotations designated "AMP" are taken from THE AMPLIFIED
BIBLE. Old Testament copyright © 1965, 1987 by the Zondervan
Corporation. The Amplified New Testament copyright © 1958, 1987 by
The Lockman Foundation. Used by permission.

Scripture quotations designated "NIV" are taken from The Holy Bible,
New International Version® NIV®. Copyright © 1973, 1978, 1984, 2011
by Biblica, Inc.™. Used by permission. All rights reserved worldwide.

Because of the dynamic nature of the Internet, any web addresses or
links contained in this book may have changed since publication and may
no longer be valid. The views expressed in this work are solely those of
the author.

This book is dedicated to all of you who hurt and feel like you will never feel okay again. Please know that God sees you right now and knows exactly what you are going through. You are not invisible and you are loved by Him more than you can ever know.

TABLE OF CONTENTS

FOREWORD

GRIEF AND SUFFERING IS AN inevitable experience we all go through in this life. The question is do we go through these trying experiences alone or with God by our side? Linda found that with Jesus she could face the profound loss of her sons and come out on the other side with hope for the future.

I knew first hand of Gary and Linda's loss of their sons as one of their pastors at that time. I officiated at both services, and at their son Matthew's service, his young faith touched many lives. Jesus said "let the little children come to me." Linda literally had to release her sons into Jesus' loving arms. Linda speaks from deep within her heart as she relates her story in this powerful book.

I highly recommend *Healing Hurts* for all who have gone through or are experiencing loss and suffering and feel lost and without hope. You will find words of encouragement that God will use to bring you through your pain and give you a future and a hope.

May God bless each of you as you read *Healing Hurts*.

—Jerry Pryor, Pastor, Army Chaplain (Retired)

INTRODUCTION

For our present troubles are small and won't last very long. Yet they produce for us a glory that vastly outweighs them and will last forever! So we don't look at the troubles we can see now; rather, we fix our gaze on things that cannot be seen. For the things we see now will soon be gone, but the things we cannot see will last forever.
2 Corinthians 4:17-18

DO YOU BELIEVE THAT SCRIPTURE passage is true?

I have to admit there have been times when I've had a hard time really believing it. My husband and I lost two children within five months of each other, and our remaining child has cerebral palsy and is in a wheelchair full-time. Let me tell you, sometimes we had a *really hard time* saying to ourselves, "Oh well, this is all going to be worth it!"

And although I know many people have had it so much worse than we have, I still have a hard time categorizing the trials we've endured as "small" like the Apostle Paul talks about above. Going through them were agonizing, and at times my heart was stripped bare.

So tell me, have you been there? Are you there right now? Do you feel at times like throwing in the towel because you just can't take it anymore?

Do you think that perhaps God has forgotten you?

I definitely have had days when it feels like the pain will never go away. The minutes and the hours drag by at a snail's pace. I start to wonder if I will ever feel okay again.

And then I look around at other people I know who are smiling and acting like they don't have a care in the world. And I start judging them—even though I really may not know them well at all. Why does it always seem like nothing bad ever happens to *them*?

As if I know what's really going on in their lives ...

Sometimes life just seems, well, cruel. You feel like every time you turn around more bad news hits. You make it through a severe illness and then you lose your job. Your mother comes to know the Lord and then your sister's child ends up getting killed. You finally reach retirement where you feel comfortable in your investments and the bottom falls out of the stock market. You and your husband finally are able to have children, and then you have a child that's disabled.

Why me?

But let me tell you, my friends, there is indeed hope. Because of the trials my husband and I have gone through, I often found myself pouring through the Scriptures trying to find morsels that might explain why all these things happened to me and my family.

And you know what? I actually found a lot—but there were moments I didn't want to listen to them!

So as you read this book, first pray that God would open your heart and mind, then hang on tight and prepare for healing. It may be hard to live through some of the things you have been trying to force out of your memory, but our God is greater than the trials and He does indeed have the answers you've been looking for.

I pray as you work your way through this short book that you will be blessed—and I pray that you will allow God's healing balm to sink deep into your soul.

Please don't ever give up, even when you feel like burying yourself in a little hole in the ground. I know I sure felt like doing that sometimes! Instead be assured that our Heavenly Father has not—*and will not*—give up on you. He desires for you to be set free from your pain and sorrow, and He will be with you every step of the way.

The healing process can sometimes really hurt, but it will all be worth it.

CHAPTER 1

MAYBE I MESSED UP TOO MUCH

Blessed be the God and Father of our Lord Jesus Christ, the Father of sympathy (pity and mercy) and the God [Who is the Source] of every comfort (consolation and encouragement), Who comforts (consoles and encourages) us in every trouble (calamity and affliction), so that we may also be able to comfort (console and encourage) those who are in any kind of trouble or distress, with the comfort (consolation and encouragement) with which we ourselves are comforted (consoled and encouraged) by God.
2 Corinthians 1:3-4 AMP

I READ THE TESTIMONY OF a lady named Grace Gonzalez one day and it broke my heart. Parts of her story reminded me of—well, me. But she definitely had gone through so much worse.

Grace had experienced a very unhappy childhood, feeling she could never do anything right.

Her little sister drowned when she was just six years old, and Grace always felt it was her fault.

When she was twelve she started using drugs and alcohol and by her mid-teens she was an addict.

She got kicked out of school when she was sixteen and left home. For the next six years she lived on the streets, landing in jail multiple times. Though Grace had heard about God, she doubted He existed.

When she was twenty-two she overdosed. When she woke up she was angry that she was still alive. She then raced off in her car hoping to end it all that way instead.

She flipped her car on the freeway and passed out.

In her semi-conscious state of awareness, she felt like flames were all around her and figured she must be in hell. She knew she deserved it.

However, a bystander pulled her out of her burning car, paramedics were called, and Grace woke up in an ambulance.

It was then that she asked God to help her, and she really meant it.

She passed out again, and when she woke up she found herself in a hospital room next to an open window with the sun shining in. She gave her life to Jesus on the spot.[1]

My sister and I grew up in a non-Christian home. Oh yes, we went to church *sometimes*, especially on Easter and Christmas. And since our mother was raised in a Lutheran church, I had to go through the confirmation process (also called Affirmation of Baptism). This she was adamant about. I hated it.

However, I grudgingly completed the requirements, and my mother was thrilled when I graduated in my white robe and received my certificate. I figured I must now be okay with God. Otherwise, why would I have had to take the course?

And like Grace Gonzalez, I also felt I could never do anything right. Whether it was trimming around the trees in the yard or scrubbing the shower stall, it always seemed like I had to go and do it again because it wasn't up to my mother's standards.

I also felt ugly—my self-esteem was really low. I had few friends. I just never fit in with the other kids at school.

Of course a lot of that could have been because I always had to wear geeky clothes which were never in style, and my bangs were always cut super short. Sports? Mom never let me participate, so I didn't have that going for me either. She always made me come right home after school.

No wonder people thought I was a loser …

Once I got out of grade school and entered junior high (called middle school these days), things seemed to get even more difficult for me. Since my maiden name was Trent a lot of the kids nicknamed me "Trenchcoat," which didn't do anything to help me feel any better about myself. I just felt unpopular and ugly.

I really can't recall whether I ever got praise for the chores I did for my mom around the house, but it could be that I've chosen to conveniently forget. Let's just say home life wasn't usually a lot of fun.

I was always much closer to my dad than my mom, so when he suffered a mental breakdown and disappeared from our lives during my teens, I started getting into way too much trouble. Rebellion was definitely a daily occurrence. Skipping classes, drinking heavily, experimenting with drugs, and doing everything I *shouldn't* became the norm for me—and I *loved it!* I now had friends. I had finally found a group of kids that I felt comfortable with.

When I finally got into high school, I found myself hating it even more than junior high. Even though I still hung out with my druggie friends (we called ourselves the "Heads"—I have no idea why), each day was becoming more and more difficult. I was getting really tired of the constant jeers from the other kids, and my grades were suffering greatly.

I started skipping classes even more often than before. Then one day when I was seventeen-years old (my junior year)—when I was actually attending class for a change—I was called to the principal's office.

As I entered his office, there sat my mom! I was busted. I had become very proficient at faking her signature on all my absentee notes, and there lying on the principal's desk was a pile of them. Mother was furious. I really couldn't blame her—she'd had her hands full since my dad had disappeared from our lives.

I dropped out of school shortly after, and found a job at a local pancake house. I absolutely *loved* that job. I worked hard learning every aspect of it that I could, and management treated me with respect. I actually *was* important after all!

And it was there at the pancake house that I also met the guy who was to become my first husband.

We became quite the item, but then one day I found out I was pregnant. Since neither of us were ready to get married or have children, he and I decided I would get an abortion. After all, it wasn't really a baby yet, right?

Yes, my thought-process was quite warped at that point in time.

About a year later we did end up getting married, and soon decided to have kids. But when I got pregnant, I ended up losing the baby in the fifth month of my pregnancy. We divorced not too long after.

I met my second and current husband a couple years later, and after we married we waited for ten years before we decided we wanted to try and start a family.

With our first pregnancy we delivered a healthy baby boy, and named him Matthew. And, about eighteen months later, I got pregnant again. That was perfect, because *my* plan was to have two boys, two years apart. That to me would be the ideal family.

Then I found out I was carrying twins. But instead of being excited and thankful, I got extremely mad at God. *How could He do this to me?* I started yelling and screaming right there in the doctor's office (certainly not in a nice way), and cursed God repeatedly during the ensuing months as I grew bigger and bigger with the babies.

The troubles started in my seventh month of pregnancy when I was scheduled to start weekly non-stress tests because the twins were identical in the same sac. The umbilical cord was shown to be wrapped around one of their necks. It was crucial that I not go into labor because the cord would tighten and cut-off the blood supply to that baby.

When I went in for my first non-stress test, almost immediately the on-call doctor started having difficulties finding the babies' heartbeats. The staff started frantically trying to contact my primary physician, and when he finally arrived he rushed me in for an emergency C-section.

Both little babies ended up being transferred to the neonatal intensive care unit (NICU) at Children's Hospital in Seattle. But sweet little Bryan, the smallest twin, was never able to get to the point where he could breathe or eat on his own. Doctors told us his brain stem was not attached correctly. So in Bryan's third month of life we had him transferred to a fragile care facility, where he passed away peacefully a few days later into the waiting arms of Jesus.

Bryan's twin brother, Jeffrey, came home from the hospital a few weeks prior to Bryan's heavenly home-going. Through our pain and grief we were so thankful for Jeffrey's big brother Matthew, who was only two-years old at the time. He absolutely loved his little brother to pieces. He would hold him, and play with him often (at least as much as a little boy can). But our thankfulness turned to an agony sharper than anything we could ever imagine when just five months after baby Bryan passed away, Matthew died in his sleep.

Matthew had always been healthy and strong, and the coroner really had no answer to explain why his death happened. He ended up writing in his report: "SIDS?"

Our world came crashing to the ground as the intenseness of that pain seeped through our pores. How could this happen? Why had God allowed it? What about Jeffrey? He needed a big brother! Then as the months passed we noticed that Jeffrey was not progressing as quickly as he should. He was later diagnosed with cerebral palsy.

I couldn't help but ask myself on more than one occasion: *Was it because of all the bad choices I had made in my life? Maybe cursing God when I found out I was pregnant with twins was the last straw?*

Ah, but God ... He accomplished many things stemming from those days of pain and agony—which I talk about in detail in my book *The God of All Comfort*.[2] The most important thing for me at that time was that I finally realized I couldn't handle life by myself. I needed Jesus. I needed help. So I surrendered my life to His saving grace.

And you know what? God *always* came through during those horrendous moments when we thought we just couldn't make it another day—sometimes in unexpected ways.

We must always remember that we're human, and God knows our frailties. We make mistakes (often!), but God is always right by us; and when we fall He is there to reach out His hand and pull us back to an upright position. With love.

There is a man in the Bible who also made some bad decisions, and one of them almost led to a whole shipload of sailors being killed. His name? Jonah.

The book of Jonah starts off in chapter one with God asking Jonah to go and tell the wicked city of Nineveh that they needed to repent and turn from their sins. If not, God was going to destroy them all.

But ...

> Jonah got up and went in the opposite direction to get away from the LORD. He went down to the port of Joppa, where he found a ship leaving for Tarshish. He bought a ticket and went on board, hoping to escape from the LORD by sailing to Tarshish. [v. 3]

One thing that is extremely important for us to learn is that when God asks us to do something, we better do it, or else there will be consequences.

And consequences there were:

> But the LORD hurled a powerful wind over the sea, causing a violent storm that threatened to break the ship apart. Fearing for their lives, the desperate sailors shouted to their gods for help and threw the cargo overboard to lighten the ship. [vv. 4-5a]

Because of Jonah's selfishness in not wanting to obey God, all the people on the ship with him were about to die a horrible death by drowning in the sea.

All because Jonah was living in disobedience to what God had asked him to do.

It's so hard to remember that our lives are not to be "all about us." Proverbs 16:18 tells us: "Pride goes before destruction, and haughtiness before a fall." What is "haughtiness"? It is showing an attitude of superiority and contempt for others that we perceive are inferior to ourselves.

God wanted Jonah to go to the Ninevites, but quite frankly Jonah just didn't like those people. He didn't want them to repent. So he decided to try and run away from God—as if any of us ever could! Psalm 139:7-12 says:

> I can never escape from your Spirit! I can never get away from your presence! If I go up to heaven, you are there; if I go down to the grave, you are there. If I ride the wings of the morning, if I dwell by the farthest oceans, even there your hand will guide me, and your strength will support me. I could ask the darkness to hide me and the light around me to become night—but even in darkness I cannot hide from you. To you the night shines as bright as day. Darkness and light are the same to you.

Nope … there's definitely no escaping the eyes of the Lord.

Back on Jonah's boat, since the sailors are afraid they are about to die, they do what was common at that time: they cast lots to figure out who on board was responsible for God pounding their vessel with the vicious storm.

Of course the lot falls on Jonah, who finally admits everything:

'Why has this awful storm come down on us?' [the sailors] demanded. 'Who are you? What is your line of work? What country are you from? What is your nationality?'

Jonah answered, 'I am a Hebrew, and I worship the LORD, the God of heaven, who made the sea and the land.'

The sailors were terrified when they heard this, for he had already told them he was running away from the LORD. 'Oh, why did you do it?' they groaned. And since the storm was getting worse all the time, they asked him, 'What should we do to you to stop this storm?'

'Throw me into the sea,' Jonah said, 'and it will become calm again. I know that this terrible storm is all my fault.' [vv. 8-12]

The sailors definitely show a lot more compassion for Jonah than he had shown them. Because even after Jonah admitted everything, they still didn't want to throw him overboard to certain death, even if his disobedience was the sole cause of their calamity. So instead they tried rowing the boat back to land, but the storm got worse.

Finally the sailors come to the realization that the only way to save any of them was to toss Jonah over the side of the boat. They take a moment to pray to the true God though they have yet to personally experience Him, and plead that He will not get mad at them for throwing Jonah into the swirling waters.

Then into the sea Jonah was thrown.

The storm immediately stopped. Think about how amazing this must have been to the men. It says in v. 16 that when the storm stopped, the men "were awestruck by the LORD's great power, and they offered him a sacrifice and vowed to serve him."

Probably, you already know what happens next. God sent a giant fish to swallow Jonah, who suddenly finds himself inside the fish's slimy belly, full of who-knows-what, for three days and three nights.

However, when we get to chapter two we find that just like Grace Gonzalez—as well as myself—when it got as bad as it could get, Jonah decides it's time to stop fooling around with God. He prays and surrenders to Him right there inside the fish's belly. The fish then spits Jonah out and he lands on dry ground.

Coming into chapter three, we find God again telling Jonah he needs to go to Nineveh, and this time Jonah obeys. He spends three days traveling throughout the city warning the people that their destruction is just around the corner. If they refuse to turn from their sins within forty days, they will cease to exist as a city.

What happens? The Ninevites turn to God, and God forgives them (vv. 6-10)!

However, going into chapter four we see that just because Jonah finally obeyed God and did what He had asked, that still doesn't mean he changed his mind about the people living in Nineveh. Our friend still had so much he needed to learn. And after God *did* change His mind about destroying the city, Jonah was *not* happy:

> This change of plans greatly upset Jonah, and he became very angry. So he complained to the LORD

about it: 'Didn't I say before I left home that you would do this, LORD? That is why I ran away to Tarshish! I knew that you are a merciful and compassionate God, slow to get angry and filled with unfailing love. You are eager to turn back from destroying people. Just kill me now, LORD! I'd rather be dead than alive if what I predicted will not happen.' [vv. 1-3]

Oh my goodness—arrogance intensified!

Then Jonah takes off and leaves Nineveh while having his own personal pity party. He goes outside the city and builds himself a little shelter. There he decides he will wait and see exactly what God is going to do with the city.

As Jonah waits, since it was so hot that day God lovingly provides him with a large shady plant to help keep him cool. That makes Jonah happy.

However, God isn't through teaching Jonah a few things:

But God also arranged for a worm! The next morning at dawn the worm ate through the stem of the plant so that it withered away. And as the sun grew hot, God arranged for a scorching east wind to blow on Jonah. The sun beat down on his head until he grew faint and wished to die. 'Death is certainly better than living like this!' he exclaimed.

Then God said to Jonah, 'Is it right for you to be angry because the plant died?'

'Yes,' Jonah retorted, 'even angry enough to die!' [vv. 7-9]

Oh my!

Friends, may we remember that God is God, and He will always have the last word:

> Then the LORD said, 'You feel sorry about the plant, though you did nothing to put it there. It came quickly and died quickly. But Nineveh has more than 120,000 people living in spiritual darkness, not to mention all the animals. Shouldn't I feel sorry for such a great city?' [vv. 10-11]

And there the book of Jonah ends. I find myself wondering whether Jonah ever got it together or not. We're not told.

But one thing this book does tell me is that there's always hope, no matter what kind of stupid things we've done—or continue doing! Lamentations 3:22-23 tells us: "The faithful love of the LORD never ends! His mercies never cease. Great is his faithfulness; his mercies begin afresh each morning."

What a great God!

Questions to Ponder

1. Have you ever found yourself thinking during times of pain that God is punishing you because of bad choices you have made in your life?

2. If so, what effect have those thoughts had on you? Have they made you mad at God, or have they caused you to instead draw closer to Him to find out the truth?

3. The apostle Paul, before becoming a Christian, was named Saul, and he did horrible things to those that believed in God, killing and imprisoning them—including women and children (Acts 8:1-3). But then one day as he was continuing his rampage, something happened which changed him drastically. What does Acts 9:3-6 say?

4. God renamed Saul of Tarsus Paul, and the Lord Jesus used him mightily to grow His church. What does Paul state in Romans 8:38-39?

5. After reading that passage, do you believe that God has that same love for you? Why or why not?

CHAPTER 2

BUT, WHY ME?

I knew you before I formed you in your mother's
womb. Before you were born I set you apart and
appointed you as my prophet to the nations.
Jeremiah 1:5

WHEN JONI EARECKSON TADA WAS 17 years old, she was just a typical teenager. However, that all changed after a diving accident which left her as a quadriplegic. And now, after almost fifty years in a wheelchair, she says getting up in the morning is still so very difficult.

> 'Every single morning when I wake up I need Jesus so badly,' she told CBN News. 'I just can't tolerate the thought of another day as a quadriplegic with someone else giving me a bed bath and exercising my legs and toileting routines ... it all just seems too overwhelming.'
>
> Her next thought ... is to pray 'Jesus, I need you. I can't do this. I cannot do quadriplegia but I can do all things through you.'[3]

If anyone has the right to say "why me?" I think Joni Eareckson Tada would be at the top of the list.

Think back to your teenage years for a moment. My sister and I used to go swimming all the time when we were younger since our mom loved to go to the beach. We dove or jumped off many diving boards. We used to jump off our boat often when we were out on the lake. I've even jumped off rock cliffs into the water (not the real tall ones like in the movies, however).

I remember sometimes I'd try to dive, but instead would do a horrendous belly-flop, hitting the water in a bad position—and it hurt! I also remember the feeling of jumping off a cliff and then sinking down deeper and deeper into the lake or river. I'd start to wonder whether I would be able to make it back up to the top before I ran out of air.

Yet I always did.

I don't ever remember thinking about hitting a rock and being knocked unconscious. I also certainly never thought I'd get hurt to the point where I could become severely disabled. Drowning? Maybe. Becoming a quadriplegic full-time in a wheelchair? Never.

I'm sure Joni never thought something like that would ever happen to her either.

So why *did* it happen to her? Why did a typical, healthy, active young woman have to suddenly be turned into a woman no longer able to take care of herself?

We certainly won't know all the answers until we get to heaven. But one thing we can be sure of: God was right there with her, and He had a purpose and a plan.

My husband and I never imagined we would have a special needs child that needed to be in a wheelchair. Most people don't. You get pregnant, do your best to stay as healthy as possible during your pregnancy, and then just assume that when the baby is born he or she will be a healthy and happy child.

And normally that's just the way it goes.

We started to think something might not be right with our surviving twin, Jeffrey, when he was still unable to sit up or even crawl when he neared the one-year-old mark. The doctors were hopeful that he was just a little delayed because of his prematurity, but as one year rolled into two, it was obvious something was not right.

A specialized children's neurologist discovered after running many tests that it appeared Jeffrey had suffered seizures either right before or right after his birth, which had created empty pockets in his brain. What that meant was that all the wires in his little brain were not functioning the way typical kids' brains function. A lot of his nerves were not connected properly. We walked out of the specialist's office with a diagnosis of cerebral palsy.

We were absolutely devastated.

As time went on we still tried to cling onto the hope that things would turn out okay. Surely eventually Jeffrey would get stronger and be able to walk, talk, and function the way other kids do.

And Jeffrey worked hard to move towards that goal. He had physical therapy, occupational therapy, and speech therapy all the way through high school.

Before he turned five years old, the physical therapists actually were able to get him to the point where he could take a few steps independently with a walker. We were so excited! Yet as he grew taller and taller, his little body just wasn't able to stand upright the way it was supposed to. He tried really hard, but eventually we had to give in and buy him his first wheelchair.

And now, as of the writing of this book, Jeffrey is in his mid-20s, and similar to Joni Eareckson Tada, he still can't go to the bathroom, take a bath, or prepare something to eat without someone helping him. He cannot dress or undress by himself. Once he's placed in his wheelchair, he is stuck there until someone comes to get him out of it, and then unless he's been placed on the floor where he can scoot a bit on his stomach, he's stuck until someone comes to put him back in his wheelchair once again.

My heart has been ripped to shreds repeatedly through the years as I've seen him struggle to try and do things that to you or I would be simple tasks. Why him? That's a question I have asked so very often.

I held back tears many times when he used to ask me when he was small why he could not walk like the other kids in his class.

I have seen him at high school dances wanting to join in and dance with his peers, but he has been unable to do so. Sometimes he would wheel himself out to the dance floor, and just spin around in his chair trying to move to the beat of the music.

I've seen him on many school field trips where he can only go so far in his chair before he's relegated to wait behind for the rest of the kids to get finished with whatever they're doing because not everywhere has been made wheelchair accessible. And I've also had teachers tell me he was unable to even *go* on some of the trips because he wouldn't be able to get around in his wheelchair at all. It hurts, and my heart would just break as I would try and explain why he could not attend—when the field trip sounded like so much fun.

Plus, Jeffrey has a hard time speaking clearly due to his cerebral palsy. When people ask him questions it crushes me to see him try so hard to answer just like anyone else. And then I watch a lot of people get so uncomfortable hearing him struggle in his stuttering that they end up turning away before he has even finished one sentence. I look at his face and wonder what he's feeling.

Also because of his disability, his sensory abilities are totally different than yours or mine. For instance, if food is still on his face after he eats, he cannot feel it there. So if someone doesn't tell him about it, he can go around all day with it on him. My husband once picked him up from a field trip while in high school and he had chocolate all over his face that he had no clue about. I was devastated—could not someone have said something?

There have been many times when his classmates have simply avoided inviting him to their parties and outings. Sometimes every-

one else in the class was invited but him. Yes, I do understand—
at the same time it still hurts. To see his face when he hears later
about the fun he missed just crushes me. He wants to belong and
have friends like everyone else. And again I ask the question, "Lord,
why did this all have to happen to him?" It just doesn't seem fair.

Sometimes I've tried to imagine how it would be for me to be in
a wheelchair like he is. And quite frankly I don't think I would have
nearly as good an attitude. As the years have gone by, Jeffrey just
seems to have come to accept that "this is the way it's supposed to
be." It is just the way God made him.

However, as we all ask ourselves the "why" question during our
times of pain, we must remember that the bottom line is that those
of us who know Jesus have been called before the foundation of the
world to be His children (John 15:16, Ephesians 1:4), and that He
has special plans for all of us who believe (Jeremiah 29:11).

And that includes Joni Eareckson Tada, Jeffrey, me, and you.

God's plans are often mysterious, certainly beyond our
comprehension.

I wonder what thoughts went through the head of a man
named Jeremiah who penned the book by the same name. Because
in chapter one, God spoke to him and said, "I knew you before I
formed you in your mother's womb. Before you were born I set you
apart and appointed you my prophet to the nations" (Jeremiah 1:5).

Ummm, say what?

Excuse me?

No way!

We don't know exactly how old he was, but Scripture does say that Jeremiah tried using excuses to get out of God's calling by trying to say he was just too young (v. 6), and then he even tried using one of the lines Moses used in claiming to not be a good enough speaker to do the job (Exodus 4:10).

Of course, Jeremiah's excuses didn't work. When God calls us to do a job, He wants us to do the job. He always has good reasons for wanting us for a particular task.

God's plan for young Jeremiah? "Today I appoint you to stand up against nations and kingdoms. Some you must uproot and tear down, destroy and overthrow. Others you must build up and plant" (v. 10).

I would say that was pretty heavy stuff, wouldn't you?

How do you think *you* would have reacted if God asked you to do those things? Would you have been excited? Proud? Scared? I don't know about you, but I probably would have been really frightened. After all, prophets were not always treated respectfully, were they? Remember John the Baptist … he was beheaded (Matthew 14:1-12)! Of course back in Jeremiah's time, John the Baptist hadn't been born yet, so thankfully Jeremiah had no knowledge of that particular event.

I also have found myself wondering what Jeremiah was actually doing when God first spoke to him as He did. It says in verse one that he was from a priestly family, so perhaps was he sitting in the temple meditating or studying God's Word? We just don't know.

But whatever he was doing at the time, I have no doubt some sort of fear and panic flooded through him quickly when God went on to explain the plans He had for him:

> Get up and prepare for action. Go out and tell them everything I tell you to say. Do not be afraid of them, or I will make you look foolish in front of them. For see, today I have made you strong like a fortified city that cannot be captured, like an iron pillar or a bronze wall. You will stand against the whole land—the kings, officials, priests, and people of Judah. They will fight you, but they will fail. For I am with you, and I will take care of you. I, the LORD, have spoken! [vv. 17-19]

I can just imagine Jeremiah thinking, *Uh-huh, right, I'm not supposed to be scared ...*

When I try to put myself in Jeremiah's position, I can easily imagine how the anxiety would be rising within me to drastic proportions as God explained His plan. *What on earth is He telling me? What's actually going to happen?*

Let me tell you, if God had told me years ago that I was going to have two young children die within five months of each other, and that our remaining child was going to be disabled, I certainly wouldn't have been feeling real warm and fuzzy!

But Jeremiah was a man who loved and obeyed God. So he began his prophetic ministry—which ended up lasting about forty years. He believed and trusted his Lord.

Was it always easy for him? Absolutely not! He's been nicknamed the "Weeping Prophet" for good reasons. He struggled with what

God asked him to do at times, hating to see how his people and his nation were being destroyed as they sank deeper and deeper into the throes of sin. Why was God allowing this hurt to come to his countrymen?

And why did God choose *him* to be the bearer of such bad news?

Sometimes Jeremiah even outright complained to God about what he was having to go through:

> LORD, you always give me justice when I bring a case before you. So let me bring you this complaint: Why are the wicked so prosperous? Why are evil people so happy?
>
> You have planted them, and they have taken root and prospered. Your name is on their lips, but you are far from their hearts.
>
> But as for me, LORD, you know my heart. You see me and test my thoughts. Drag these people away like sheep to be butchered! Set them aside to be slaughtered!
>
> How long must this land mourn? Even the grass in the fields has withered. The wild animals and birds have disappeared because of the evil in the land. For the people have said, 'The LORD doesn't see what's ahead for us!' …
>
> LORD, you know what's happening to me. Please step in and help me. Punish my persecutors! Please give me time; don't let me die young. It's for your sake that I am suffering.

When I discovered your words, I devoured them. They are my joy and my heart's delight, for I bear your name, O LORD God of Heaven's Armies.

I never joined the people in their merry feasts. I sat alone because your hand was on me. I was filled with indignation at their sins.

Why then does my suffering continue? Why is my wound so incurable? Your help seems as uncertain as a seasonal brook, like a spring that has gone dry. [12:1-4, 15:15-18]

Yet in spite of Jeremiah's complaints, he kept trusting God and His providence, even when things didn't make sense.

Jeremiah also wrote the book of Lamentations, which details even further the sorrow and grief he had to go through—yet is also filled with hope.

In chapter three of Lamentations, you read of a time when Jeremiah was again pouring out his heart to God. Basically he was asking, "Why me?" But even through his pain and grief he acknowledges that even though he doesn't totally understand God and His ways, he chooses to trust Him:

It is because of the Lord's mercy *and* loving-kindness that we are not consumed, because His [tender] compassions fail not ...

They are new every morning; great *and* abundant is Your stability *and* faithfulness ...

The Lord is my portion *or* share, says my living being
(my inner self); therefore will I hope in Him *and* wait
expectantly for Him ...

The Lord is good to those who wait hopefully *and*
expectantly for Him, to those who seek Him [inquire of
and for Him and require Him by right of necessity and
on the authority of God's word]. [vv. 22-25 AMP]

Bottom line: God is God, and His ways are often not something
we can visualize or comprehend. That's why normally He does not
lay out His plans for us as He did with Jeremiah, because He knows
we would panic. It is just our human nature.

Joni Eareckson Tada is one of my heroes. I wonder how she
would have responded to God if He had told her in advance that
He was planning on making her a paraplegic for the majority of
her life?

Questions to Ponder

1. It says in Jeremiah 1:5 that God had plans for Jeremiah even before he was born. How does Psalm 139:13-16 add to that?

2. The book of Ephesians was written to help us better understand God's eternal purpose, as well as the grace He has bestowed upon us. What does Ephesians 1:4-8 tell us?

3. In Jeremiah 18:1-4 the Lord tells the prophet to go down to a potter's house. What does Jeremiah see once he gets there?

4. Romans 9:20-21 also speaks about a potter. What does it say?

5. Okay, now is the time when some of you are probably saying: "Some things just aren't fair!" No, life doesn't seem fair sometimes, does it? The question is, do you trust that God has everything in His control? Why or why not?

CHAPTER 3

FORGIVENESS EVEN WHEN YOU DON'T DESERVE IT

I have been crucified with Christ and I no longer live, but Christ lives in me. The life I live in the body, I live by faith in the Son of God, who loved me and gave himself for me.
Galatians 2:20 NIV

BACK IN THE 1980'S, KARLA Faye Tucker and her boyfriend were high on drugs. Their simple plan was to steal a motorcycle from Karla Faye's best friend. Instead they ended up killing her best friend's husband and one other person with a pickaxe.

Karla Faye was sentenced to death.

A few weeks prior to her execution she was interviewed by Larry King, who asked her if she was fearful of her upcoming death.

Her reply? "No. It gets a little more exciting every day."

Why did she answer like that? Because while in prison, Karla Faye got introduced to Jesus.

Karla Faye had attended a puppet show put on by a church ministry, and was so moved that she went back to her prison cell and started reading a Bible she had stolen.

Her words:

> That night I started reading the Bible. I didn't know what I was reading and before I knew it, I was just—I was in the middle of my floor on my knees and I was just asking God to forgive me.

Of course Larry King thought for sure it had to be something more than just God who had changed her attitude, but he was totally wrong.

Karla Faye continued:

> It's called the joy of the Lord. I don't—when you have done something that I have done, like what I have done, and you have been forgiven for it, and you're loved, that has a way of so changing you. I mean, I have experienced real love. I know what real love is. I know what forgiveness is, even when I did something so horrible. I know that because God forgave me and I accepted what Jesus did on the cross. When I leave here, I am going to go be with him.[4]

Karla Faye was a real life example of someone who didn't care if people thought she was a fool—she was speaking out for Jesus with her remaining time on earth. Yes, there were severe consequences that she had to pay for her previous actions (she was executed), but she knew that after death she would truly be free.

Think about one of the worst things you think you have ever done. It could be anything: lying, stealing, inflicting harm on a person, abortion, cheating, cursing God, gossiping—anything. Do you find yourself often reliving those times, feeling guilty about your actions? Do you feel like maybe you stepped so far over the line back then that God could never forgive you?

After all, why should He since you can't forgive yourself?

Well, stop it! Don't let your mind play games with you; and don't let the enemy keep hounding you with, "You really blew it that time!" Just look at Karla Faye.

Back in chapter one, I wrote briefly about many things that I'm not proud of. No, I never murdered anyone, but I definitely was not a nice person.

In my teen years I back-stabbed people who were nice to me, I stole all sorts of stuff from stores on a regular basis, I experimented with different drugs, I drank heavily, had an abortion, and my best friend's mother and aunt were witches (yes, really).

Now I look back and wish I could erase all those things, but back then I really felt like it wasn't that big of a deal. I mean, I wasn't the only one doing that stuff, right? All my friends did those things too. My frame of mind was that I needed to participate in those things in order to get what I wanted—as well as to fit in with the cool crowd of friends I wanted to hang out with (my perception).

Oh, I could certainly lay on "niceness" when I needed to, but for the most part I was totally manipulative. I just wanted people to give me what I wanted them to give me!

Even after my husband Gary and I got married, I was still not often very nice. Oh, I loved *him* to pieces; it was others that I still was mean to, especially if they didn't agree with the way I thought things should be done.

However, I believe the *coup de grâce* was when I was told I was pregnant with twins. You see, God was supposed to be following *my* plan of having two boys, two years apart—and that did *not* include twins.

Instead of being excited and thankful when the doctor gave my husband and me the news of two precious babies growing within me, I got extremely mad at God. I cursed God repeatedly during the following months, as my stomach grew bigger and bigger with the babies.

Then in my seventh-month of pregnancy came the emergency C-section. A few months after that we lost one of the twins, and five months later our healthy two-year-old son Matthew died in his sleep. The pain was horrific, but it took that for me to really discover who Jesus was. He became real to me during that time, and I can certainly agree with Karla Faye's words that now I know without a doubt that God has forgiven me for all the wrongs I have committed, and that His love for me is real and true.

Now we're going to look at a man in the Bible—an Apostle no less—who was badder than bad. His name? Paul.

The Apostle Paul (originally named Saul) was born in a city called Tarsus. His parents were said to be strict Pharisees, and somewhat wealthy. When he was fourteen years old he was sent to a prominent teacher named Gamaliel to be trained as a Rabbi.

Paul was a man of firm convictions, and had a fiery temperament. When he felt something was not right, he acted upon it. Right was right, and wrong was wrong—final answer.

So when he was confronted with a religion (now called Christianity) he believed was heretical to Judaism, he went after everyone who followed that religion with a vengeance.[5]

Saul himself gave approval to stone the Apostle Stephen to death (Acts 7:54-8:1), and after that he went on a rampage, going house to house and dragging to prison men and women who were following the teachings of Jesus.

He readily admits in Acts 22:4 that before he understood who Jesus was, he persecuted followers of Christianity to their death. In Acts 26:9-11 he says it did not bother him when many imprisoned for their faith were killed, and even tried at times to force people into professing faith in Jesus just so they could be punished. No, he was not a nice person at all.

But one day something amazing happened.

This particular day started out quite normal—for Paul, that is:

> … Saul [Paul] was uttering threats with every breath
> and was eager to kill the Lord's followers. So he went
> to the high priest. He requested letters addressed to the

synagogues in Damascus, asking for their cooperation in the arrest of any followers of the Way [Christianity] he found there. He wanted to bring them—both men and women—back to Jerusalem in chains.

As he was approaching Damascus on this mission, a light from heaven suddenly shone down around him. He fell to the ground and heard a voice saying to him, 'Saul! Saul! Why are you persecuting me?'

'Who are you, lord?' Saul asked.

And the voice replied, 'I am Jesus, the one you are persecuting! Now get up and go into the city, and you will be told what you must do.'

The men traveling with Saul stood speechless; for they heard the sound of someone's voice but saw no one! Saul picked himself up off the ground, but when he opened his eyes he was blind. So his companions led him by the hand to Damascus. He remained there blind for three days and did not eat or drink. [Acts 9:1-9]

Meanwhile, in Damascus there lived one of Jesus's disciples named Ananias, and Jesus told him in a vision about Paul and where he was staying. The Lord told Ananias He wanted him to go to Paul, and lay his hands upon him so Paul's sight could be restored.

Ananias wasn't real thrilled about the mission God was sending him on:

'But Lord,' exclaimed Ananias, 'I've heard many people talk about the terrible things this man has done to the believers in Jerusalem! And he is authorized by the leading priests to arrest everyone who calls upon your name.'

But the Lord said, 'Go, for Saul is my chosen instrument to take my message to the Gentiles and to kings, as well as to the people of Israel. And I will show him how much he must suffer for my name's sake.'

So Ananias went and found Saul. He laid his hands on him and said, 'Brother Saul, the Lord Jesus, who appeared to you on the road, has sent me so that you might regain your sight and be filled with the Holy Spirit.' Instantly something like scales fell from Saul's eyes, and he regained his sight. Then he got up and was baptized. Afterward he ate some food and regained his strength. [Acts 9:13-19]

Although Ananias was scared he obeyed God, and that was the beginning of a powerful ministry for Paul. He ended up writing thirteen books of the New Testament, and God used him to spread the gospel to not only the Jewish people, but also to Gentiles.

But did Paul get off scot-free for all the wrong things he did? No, not at all. Here is his testimony from 2 Corinthians 11:23-27:

... I have worked much harder, been put in prison more often, been whipped times without number, faced death again and again. Five different times the Jewish leaders gave me thirty-nine lashes. Three times I was beaten with rods. Once I was stoned. Three times I was shipwrecked. Once I spent a whole night and a day adrift at sea. I have traveled on many long journeys. I have faced danger from rivers and from robbers. I have faced danger from my own people, the Jews, as well as from the Gentiles. I have faced danger in the cities, in the deserts, and on the seas. And I have faced danger from men who claim to be believers but are not. I have worked hard and long, enduring many sleepless nights. I have been hungry and thirsty and have often gone without food. I have shivered in the cold, without enough clothing to keep me warm.

However, none of that mattered to Paul because he had finally found truth in Jesus, and Jesus had set him free (John 8:32).

Questions to Ponder

1. Take a look again at Galatians 2:20 which starts out this chapter. What do these words Paul penned really mean to you?

2. Do you believe God has your situation in control? Write down Jeremiah 29:11-13.

3. In your mind, Paul may have deserved all the beatings and pain he endured once he came to truly know Jesus. Yet what does he write in 1 Timothy 1:13?

4. Paul had warped thinking about who God was because of his schooling spoken about earlier in this chapter. But once he realized the error of his ways, he repented and turned his life around. Did that mean he was now perfect? Look up Romans 7:15-20.

5. Perhaps you already know Jesus, and you still find yourself messing up. You wonder and worry if God is going to really make you pay this time. But 1 John 1:9 says once we confess our sins, God forgives us. What does Romans 8:1 say?

CHAPTER 4

SUFFERING WHEN YOU ARE DOING GOOD

And we know that in all things God works for the good of those who love Him, who have been called according to His purpose.
Romans 8:28 NIV

AMY CARMICHAEL WAS BORN IN Ireland and raised by Christian parents. As she grew into adulthood, she felt called to go into missions.

Her call, however, came in a couple very unique ways.

One time as she and her family were leaving church she saw an old beggar woman come staggering out of an alley. Amy's heart went out to her, so she and her brother went and helped the woman.

Suddenly she spotted some people from their church heading their way. Amy was embarrassed so she tried to hide. It was then she heard a voice in her head saying "Gold, silver, precious stones, wood, hay and straw—the fire will test what sort of work each has

done. If the foundation survives, he will receive the reward." She went home and searched her Bible, finding those same words in 1 Corinthians 3:12. Amy then knelt by her bed, and promised God that in the future she would only do things that pleased Him.

Another time she and her mother stopped to have tea and biscuits in a restaurant. As they ate, Amy saw a dirty little beggar girl outside pressing her nose against the window. The poor little girl, who obviously was hungry, touched Amy so much that she made another promise—that when she grew up she would give her money to the poor.[6]

Amy ended up serving the majority of her life as a missionary in South India, spending over fifty years in the Dohnavur village on a mission which came to be known as Dohnavur Fellowship. It was there that she ministered to hundreds of girls originally dedicated to becoming Hindu temple prostitutes.[7]

However, one day Amy fell, badly hurting her hip and back. Because of those injuries, the last twenty years of her life were spent confined to her bedroom in constant pain. But God had a plan. It was during those last years that she did all her writing—poems, devotional books, and accounts of her ministry, which had turned into a haven for homeless children.[8]

How Amy's life ended up just didn't seem fair, did it? Here she was devoted to missionary work—loving children with the love of Jesus. So why did she have to spend the last twenty years of her life lying in bed with so much pain?

One of the study questions ending the last chapter was regarding Jeremiah 29:11-13, which says God has plans to prosper and not harm us; and plans to give us hope and a future. Yet when you look at Amy's life, it just doesn't seem to make sense.

Growing up I often thought life was totally unfair.

I thought it unfair when my family and I moved from our home where I had some really good friends to a city where everyone seemed snobbish and had lots of money—except us. I lived feeling shunned because I didn't have the most fashionable clothes. It seemed I never fit in, except with the wrong crowd. I hardly ever got invited to any parties with my peers, but even on those few occasions when I did get invited, my mother wouldn't let me go.

I thought it unfair when my dad got laid-off from his great job of many years and had trouble finding another one. Then he suffered a mental breakdown and disappeared from our lives forever when I was just a young teenager. I loved him so much, and really didn't get along very well with my mother. Why did that have to happen? Why to him?

My husband Gary and I certainly thought it was unfair when two of our young sons died at an early age within five months of each other. We loved our boys and wanted to be the best parents we possibly could. The news is always full of parents who neglect and abuse their children. We hear of mothers who continue to drink heavily or take drugs while pregnant, causing their babies to be born with fetal alcohol syndrome—or worse. It just didn't seem right.

It certainly still seems unfair that our remaining son Jeffrey has quadriplegic cerebral palsy and has to work so hard to do even the simplest things. When he was in grade school I used to watch the other kids on the playground running around laughing and playing with their friends, while Jeffrey usually sat alienated and all alone.

It was also unfair as I dealt with my broken heart often watching Jeffrey doing his homework typing everything with just one finger on his left hand. He so wanted to do well, excel at school, and be recognized for the great kid that he was.

And it was unfair that almost every night after school I had to take him to some sort of therapy, rather than him being able to attend sports functions or gatherings like his peers did.

No, life really isn't fair, is it? I am sure you have many stories as well.

We certainly cannot go any further in the "it's not fair" theory without looking at the great man Job, who has a whole book dedicated to him in the Bible.

Who was Job? Start off reading Job chapter one, and you'll find out right away. Words used to describe him in the NIV Bible include blameless, upright, and a man who turned away from evil.

He was also very rich and had ten children.

And like any good parent he worried about his kids, so he regularly sacrificed a burnt offering for each of them, "just in case" one of them had messed up. He loved them, and wanted to do whatever he could to make sure they were all right with God.

Remember, this was Old Testament times—back before direct access to God's throne of grace was available through Jesus' death on the cross (Matthew 27:51, Hebrews 4:16).

But the enemy of this world, Satan, does not like it when people are sold-out to God, so he will do what he can to hurt us and try to get us sidetracked in our walks of faith.

As we continue reading the first chapter of Job, we see that Satan comes before God, and asks Him to give permission to hurt Job in a horrible manner by allowing him to take away basically everything he owned—including killing all his children. God says okay.

It's certainly hard to wrap our minds around all that, isn't it?

But how did Job react after that all happened? He tore his robe, shaved his head (signs of deep mourning), and fell to the ground in worship! Verse 22 says, "In all of this, Job did not sin by blaming God."

It takes a much greater person than I to endure such tragedy and not sin or get mad at God.

But there's more.

You see, Job's response to his devastating losses did not make Satan happy, so as we head into chapter two, we see that he again goes before God, and this time he wants to hurt Job physically. God again gives permission, but says he must not kill him.

Satan then afflicts Job with painful sores from the soles of his feet to the top of his head. His wife gets to the point where she's had enough, and tells Job he should curse God. His response: "No."

Verse 10 states: "... 'You talk like a foolish woman. Should we accept only good things from the hand of God, and never anything bad?' So in all this, Job said nothing wrong."

Could you have said the words Job said after all that had happened? I'm sure I couldn't!

Shortly after all those events took place, three of Job's "friends" decide they're going to visit him to sympathize and give comfort, just as friends should; however, when they actually set eyes on him they're shocked—they barely recognize him. They begin to cry, and end up sitting on the ground next to Job without speaking for seven days.

Entering into chapter three, we finally see that Job is truly human after all. He gets to the point where he's at the end of his rope. He just can't take it anymore. Why has God left him? His heart begins to unravel. Why was he born in the first place? His peace is gone, and now his days are filled with only pain, suffering and turmoil.

Job is at the lowest point in his life, no doubt about it. He begins to unload on his friends, wanting someone just to listen to him. But, as you continue reading, you'll find that (as often happens) people who have never experienced the same type of pain and grief we're currently going through will often try to make us feel better by telling us their opinions on why the bad things have happened in our lives.

Unfortunately they typically have no idea whatsoever.

That's what happened to Job. After he finishes explaining the hurts of his heart in chapter three, his friends decide it's their turn to start "helping" Job understand his severe trials. But instead they end up wounding him even more deeply.

In chapter four, Job's friend Eliphaz starts out speaking kindly to Job, but suddenly his kindness takes a turn:

> 'In the past you have encouraged many people; you have strengthened those who were weak.
>
> Your words have supported those who were falling; you encouraged those with shaky knees.
>
> But now when trouble strikes, you lose heart. You are terrified when it touches you.
>
> Doesn't your reverence for God give you confidence? Doesn't your life of integrity give you hope?
>
> Stop and think! Do the innocent die? When have the upright been destroyed?
>
> My experience shows that those who plant trouble and cultivate evil will harvest the same.
>
> A breath from God destroys them. They vanish in a blast of his anger.' [vv. 3-9]

In other words, *"Job, since you're such a good person you shouldn't be getting so worked up about all this. You should know that God will take care of you."*

Perhaps if Eliphaz would have ended right there it might have been okay. However, as you continue reading chapters four and five, you see that Eliphaz *doesn't* finish his diatribe right there, but goes on to say he also has some dreams he wants to share with Job.

If I were in Job's situation, I doubt I would be in the mood to listen to Eliphaz's dreams. And, unfortunately, telling Job his dreams did even more harm. The dreams of Eliphaz ended up hammering poor Job straight into the ground.

Why didn't he keep his mouth shut?

Job, however, speaks up in chapters six and seven after Eliphaz' speech and begins defending himself. He begs God to show him if he has sinned and pleads with Him to turn his kindness back on him. Why is God not speaking to him in his misery?

Job is hurting, and he is hurting badly. But instead of sympathy, one of his other friends, Bildad, begins his own hurtful rant in chapter eight:

> 'How long will you go on like this? You sound like a blustering wind.
>
> Does God twist justice? Does the Almighty twist what is right?
>
> Your children must have sinned against him, so their punishment was well deserved.
>
> But if you pray to God and seek the favor of the Almighty,
>
> And if you are pure and live with integrity, he will surely rise up and restore your happy home.' [vv. 2-6]

Ouch, with a friend like that, who needs enemies?

After Job again pleads for mercy from God in chapters nine and ten, Job's third friend Zophar gets in the act as we reach chapter eleven. And if you thought Eliphaz and Bildad were uncaring and cruel, you probably shouldn't even *read* the words Zophar says as he cuts further into Job's already deeply wounded heart.

Continuing on in the book of Job, you will find that over and over again Job tries to keep his focus on God and not listen to his "friends," but it gets harder and harder. People and their words sometimes cut so deep to the bone that all you want to do is slam the door on them, then run away and hide.

Have you been there? I have. People and their words were some of the hardest things for my husband and me, particularly after losing our healthy two-year old son, Matthew. Well-meaning friends and others who knew us would offer their perceived knowledge of why he had died suddenly:

"You must have sin in your life," some would say.

Yeah, definitely thought of that one.

Others would pipe in with: "There must've been something going on inside his body that you didn't know of."

Well, "DUH" I wanted to scream sometimes.

Another line we heard often: "At least you still have Jeffrey."

But what about Matthew? We miss him! Jeffrey needs his brother!

Sometimes I really felt like saying, "How would you feel if you lost one of your kids and your remaining kids no longer had a brother or sister to play with? You're not helping us feel better!"

Yes, the enemy of our souls definitely used the words people said to beat us up often. And especially for me, I often felt that losing our boys had all happened because of the dumb things I used to do.

But we must remember there are *always* reasons why God allows tragedies to happen in our lives, and often we will not find out totally why they've occurred until we get to heaven. We just must trust Him.

God had a purpose for Job having to endure such severe trials, even if Job didn't understand it at the time. And God ended up blessing Job afterwards with even more than he had previously.

Job's story reminds me of a short article I read years ago in a Campus Crusade for Christ magazine (now called "Cru"). The article was about a married couple who were blessed with four children. They lived in a small old house, and couldn't afford anything larger. So they sought prayer support from many people, asking them to pray if the Lord might help them be able to afford a larger home.

God did answer their prayer, and it certainly was in a way they never expected.

One day when the whole family was out, their house burned totally to the ground. The husband was very angry at God and told him so—more than once. However, the wife kept her faith and discovered a cross which had somehow gotten etched into the charred remains of their home. To her this was a message from their Lord, telling them, "I'm here; I'm in control. This isn't an accident. Just watch what I'm going to do."

Sure enough, a couple days later they received news from their insurance company that because of the fine exquisite detailing of their now destroyed house which had been built years before, they were to be awarded a sum of money far greater than the face value of their property! This enabled them to move into a beautifully designed, roomy home they never could have afforded if God hadn't intervened. The lesson this couple learned was that sometimes God must blast before He builds.

Questions to Ponder

1. Look up Romans 8:28. Do you believe what it says? Why or why not?

2. In Job 38, God speaks personally to Job. But God's first words to him must have cut him to the core. What do verses 2-4 say?

3. The Lord continues speaking through chapter forty-one, but then allows Job to respond. What does Job say to God in 42:2-3?

4. Job definitely exhibited great faith. Though he had trembled and faltered at times, he realized his utter helplessness, and knew he could do nothing but keep trusting God. Jesus also faced extreme pain and anguish, yet what did He pray in Matthew 26:39?

5. We will never be able to understand all God's ways—they are not our own! Yet God takes care of us. In Job 42:7-17 God rebukes Eliphaz, yet then says He'll have Job pray for them. After that, what was God's ultimate blessing for Job in 42:10-16?

HAS GOD FORGOTTEN ME?

For our present troubles are small and won't last very long. Yet they produce for us a glory that vastly outweighs them and will last forever.
2 Corinthians 4:17

JOHN SIDNEY MCCAIN III WAS just a young man when the Vietnam War broke out. He followed in the footsteps of his dad and grandfather by volunteering for the military, serving the country he loved. He began flying attack planes on low-altitude bombing runs against the North Vietnamese.

However, on October 26, 1967—during his 23rd air mission— McCain's plane was shot down over the North Vietnamese capital of Hanoi. He broke both arms and one leg during the crash.

He was then captured and eventually taken to Hoa Loa prison, nicknamed the "Hanoi Hilton."[9] But it was certainly *not* a plush hotel.

McCain ended up spending five and a half years in various prison camps; three and a half of those years were spent in solitary confinement. McCain and the other prisoners were repeatedly beaten and tortured—often for hours—as an incentive to provide classified information.

McCain did his best to hold on to his faith through those years, but there were times when it seemed as though he would never be set free.

There were, however, a few bright spots. One time while he was tied very tightly with ropes in solitary confinement, a guard quietly appeared, loosened his bonds, and quickly left. Hours later, the same guard reappeared and tightened the ropes again, obviously in an attempt to hide his earlier act of mercy.

McCain spotted this same guard occasionally in the following months, but the guard never would look at him. Until something happened one Christmas morning.

That day McCain was taken out of his cell and allowed to stand outside for a few minutes. Suddenly that same guard came over to McCain, and using his foot drew a cross in the dirt. Then the guard stood with him for just a moment, erased the cross and walked away once again.

McCain stated that the experience with that prison guard gave him what he needed to keep his faith, and helped him to become a better, stronger, and more faithful man.[10]

You see, God knew *exactly* where John McCain was, and had not forgotten him.

I once had a beautiful friend (who now lives up in heaven) who shared with a small group of ladies of a time when she totally felt forgotten by God.

Like Gary and I, she and her husband were also raising a child with cerebral palsy. Their daughter was in a wheelchair as well, and could only do minimal things with her arms, hands, and legs.

If you have cared for someone with a disability you know how difficult it can be. The days roll into months, which then turn into years. It seems as though every day is the same as you find yourself dealing with your child's needs and attending unending doctor and therapy appointments. You get so tired sometimes—emotionally and physically.

God, are you there? Do you see me? Do you really care?

My friend tried to keep as upbeat as she could, and whenever I would see her at church or around town she wouldn't hesitate to give me a big hug and share encouraging words to help brighten my day.

But as the years went on, she began experiencing physical pains of her own. Most of the pain was in her back, which the doctors said was most likely caused by lifting her daughter in and out of her wheelchair for so many years.

Then came times when it was hard for her to even walk because she hurt so badly.

It finally got to the point where some days all she could do was lie in bed all day long because her back pain was so intense.

Then the pain started in other parts of her body. Her doctor took some tests and discovered she had cancer, and it appeared to be spreading quickly. The prognosis was not good, but she still did her best to put a smile on her face—at least in public.

However, that day in the ladies group she shared with us that when she was at home all alone she would often experience extreme loneliness and despair. At times it just seemed to seep through every pore of her being.

One beautiful day she went out to sit on her back deck, and started crying out to God. She wasn't angry at Him; she just needed to talk and get things off her chest.

God, have you forgotten me?

Suddenly as she was sitting there weeping softly, she saw a small bird fly close to her on the deck. The bird sat on one of the ledges and just seemed to look at her for a while. It reminded her of the gospel song "His Eye is on the Sparrow" which she began singing softly to herself:

> Why should I feel discouraged
> Why should the shadows come
> Why should my heart be lonely
> And long for heaven and home
> When Jesus is my portion
> My constant friend is He
> His eye is on the sparrow
> And I know he watches me
> His eye is on the sparrow
> And I know he watches me[11]

She shared that she felt such peace come over her. She knew she was *not* forgotten. She felt God was right there with her, and that He was telling her he loved her more than she could imagine.

My friend's story reminded me of Jesus's words in the book of Matthew. He had just named the twelve disciples, and had given them supernatural power and authority to heal and drive out evil spirits. He told them they were to travel and share the good news of the gospel, and they were not to take anything with them, including money or extra clothes.

And if those instructions alone weren't enough to overpower their minds a bit, Jesus then told them they also needed to be on guard against evil men who would try to throw them in prison and beat them. But He also told them to not be afraid!

Take a look:

> Do not be afraid of those who want to kill your body; they cannot touch your soul. Fear only God, who can destroy both soul and body in hell. What is the price of two sparrows—one copper coin? *But not a single sparrow can fall to the ground without your Father knowing it.* And the very hairs on your head are all numbered. *So don't be afraid; you are more valuable to God than a whole flock of sparrows.* [Matthew 10:28-31, emphasis mine]

Yes, my friend was discouraged and a little frightened of what the future held. We're all human, and when life keeps beating us down—or the unknown comes blasting at us—it's normal. But remember that God always knows where we are.

There's a young man in the Bible named Joseph who certainly experienced rejection, pain, and loneliness. We start learning about him in Genesis 37.

That chapter tells us about Jacob and his sons. Joseph was the youngest son, and Jacob's favorite. This made his brothers very jealous. I'm sure their envy grew to even greater proportions after Jacob gave Joseph alone a beautiful ornamental robe.

Later on, something happens, and Joseph just cannot wait to tell it to his older brothers. What was it? Let's look at what the Bible says:

> One night Joseph had a dream, and when he told his brothers about it, they hated him more than ever. 'Listen to this dream,' he said. 'We were out in the field tying up bundles of grain. Suddenly my bundle stood up, and your bundles all gathered around and bowed low before mine!' [vv. 5-7]

Hmmm—so was Joseph saying that in time all his brothers were going to be bowing down to him? Sounds a little arrogant on Joseph's part, don't you think? Needless to say this didn't go over well.

Then to add fuel to the fire, Joseph has another dream almost identical to his first one. But in this dream not only his brothers are bowing down to him, but also his dad! How does his father react?

> This time he told the dream to his father as well as to his brothers, but his father scolded him. 'What kind of

dream is that?' he asked. Will your mother and I and your brothers actually come and bow to the ground before you?' But while his brothers were jealous of Joseph, his father wondered what the dreams meant. [vv. 10-11]

Time goes on, and then one day Jacob decides to send Joseph to check on his brothers, who were traveling with their flocks a distance from their home. Why did he send Joseph? We're not exactly sure, but to me it didn't seem like a very good decision. After all, shouldn't Jacob have been observant enough to tell that his other sons were insanely jealous of Joseph?

Yet Joseph is obedient, and takes off—of course wearing the beautiful robe that his dad had made for him. He finds out where his brothers with their flocks are grazing, and starts heading in that direction.

His brothers spot him coming, and their jealousy and hatred come bubbling to the surface at a rapid pace. All but one brother decide they want to kill him; but instead they end up taking Joseph's coat off, and then throwing him into a cistern. When some travelers heading to Egypt come by, they decide to sell Joseph to them. Why not make some money off him—if they just kill him they'll gain nothing!

After Joseph has been sold off, the brothers devise a scheme to fool their father, and indeed their father is fooled, his heart broken by his wicked conniving sons:

Then the brothers killed a young goat and dipped Joseph's robe in its blood. They sent the beautiful robe to their father with this message: 'Look at what we found. Doesn't this robe belong to your son?'

Their father recognized it immediately. 'Yes,' he said, 'it is my son's robe. A wild animal must have eaten him. Joseph has clearly been torn to pieces!' Then Jacob tore his clothes and dressed himself in burlap. He mourned deeply for his son for a long time. His family all tried to comfort him, but he refused to be comforted. 'I will go to my grave mourning for my son,' he would say, and then he would weep. [vv. 31-35]

But what actually happened to Joseph? Where did he end up?

The story picks back up in Genesis 39, where we see that Joseph is still alive. He has been sold as a slave to Potiphar, one of Pharaoh's high-ranking officials. But God blesses Joseph while he is there as Potiphar's slave, giving him favor with Potiphar to the extent that Joseph is entrusted with taking care of the whole household (vv. 1-6a).

What a great ending to the story! Or, not …

Joseph had grown up to become quite handsome, and he caught the eye of Potiphar's wife, which wasn't a good thing. Potiphar's wife decides she wants him for her own personal pleasure! She asks Joseph to come to bed with her one day:

But Joseph refused. 'Look,' he told her, 'my master trusts me with everything in his entire household. No one here has more authority than I do. He has held back nothing from me except you, because you are his wife. How could I do such a wicked thing? It would be a great sin against God.'

She kept putting pressure on Joseph day after day, but he refused to sleep with her, and he kept out of her way as much as possible. [vv. 8-10]

Ew, a woman scorned—you know what they say about that! Let's read on:

One day, however, no one else was around when he went in to do his work. She came and grabbed him by his cloak, demanding, 'Come on, sleep with me!' Joseph tore himself away, but he left his cloak in her hand as he ran from the house.

When she saw that she was holding his cloak in her hand and he had fled, she called out to her servants. Soon all the men came running. 'Look!' she said. 'My husband has brought this Hebrew slave here to make fools of us! He came into my room to rape me, but I screamed. When he heard me scream, he ran outside and got away, but he left his cloak behind with me.'

She kept the cloak with her until her husband came home. Then she told him her story. 'That Hebrew slave you've brought into our house tried to come in and fool around with me,' she said. 'But when I screamed, he ran outside, leaving his cloak with me!' [vv. 11-18]

I find myself often wondering just how much of his wife's story Potiphar and her servants *really* believed. Yet whether true or not, Potiphar ends up throwing Joseph in prison.

Poor Joseph! But again God gives him favor, and the prison warden ends up putting Joseph in charge of all the prison's operations. "The warden had no more worries, because Joseph took care of everything. The LORD was with him and caused everything he did to succeed" (v. 23).

One day it really *does* seem as though things are about to change for our Joseph.

As we head into chapter forty, Pharaoh's cupbearer and baker are thrown into the same prison where Joseph is located. One night both of them have individual dreams, which neither of them understand.

When Joseph sees them the next morning, he knows something is wrong, so he asks them. They tell him they need an interpreter for their dreams.

Joseph tells them that God is the Grand Interpreter, and asks them to tell him their dreams. They do so.

The Lord allows Joseph to correctly interpret the dreams, and Joseph asks the cupbearer—who was reinstated to his position a few days later—to please remember him before Pharaoh as he had been falsely imprisoned and would like to be set free.

But what happens next? The cupbearer forgets all about Joseph's kindness once he gets his position back (v. 23), so Joseph ends up remaining in prison.

I can't help but think about what was possibly going through Joseph's mind through all those years. Scripture doesn't specifically say.

The Bible certainly doesn't say he sat in his cell whining, and it also doesn't say that he cursed God or questioned Him. So did he spend his days praying? Praising God? I hope to ask him someday.

As we come to chapter forty-one (two years later), Pharaoh himself has two dreams, and he doesn't understand either one. The call goes out for an interpreter. All of a sudden the cupbearer remembers Joseph and how he had accurately interpreted his own dream while *he* had been in prison.

Joseph is brought before Pharaoh, and God gives him the wisdom to correctly interpret Pharaoh's dreams.

What were they about? A severe famine that was soon going to come upon the land which would last for seven years.

Joseph has a plan in his head as he speaks with Pharaoh. He begins to lay out how he believes the kingdom can make it through the famine.

I *love* this:

> Joseph's suggestions were well received by Pharaoh and all his officials. So Pharaoh asked his officials, 'Can we find anyone else like this man so obviously filled with the spirit of God?' Then Pharaoh said to Joseph, 'Since God has revealed the meaning of the dreams to you, clearly no one else is as intelligent or wise as you are. You will be in charge of my court, and all my people will take orders from you. *Only I, sitting on my throne, will have a rank higher than yours'.* [vv. 37-40, emphasis mine]

Yes, Pharaoh puts Joseph in charge of his whole palace!

So going back to the beginning of Joseph's story, do you not think that God gave Joseph an inkling of what was to come way back when he was a young man and had his dreams? For it turned out that through Joseph's wisdom under Pharaoh, Egypt and the surrounding countries were saved from a terrible famine.

God used all those years of Joseph's life after being sold by his brothers to shape and mold him for what was to come.

But what about Joseph's brothers and father Jacob? What happened to them?

In chapters forty-two through forty-five, we see that because the famine had become so severe, Jacob eventually sends his sons to Egypt to buy grain—and they end up face-to-face with Joseph! They don't realize it's him at first because he now dresses and looks more like an Egyptian. However, once he makes his true identity known, his brothers "were terrified" (45:3 NIV).

Joseph had really learned a lot through his painful growing years, and Genesis 46 through 50 gives us a glimpse of true love at its finest. Joseph forgives his brothers, and ends up taking care of his whole family.

He's also later reunited with his father, and the family is provided choice land close to where Joseph himself resides under Pharaoh's care. Never will they need to worry about food again.

So Joseph's dreams did indeed come true, but certainly *not* in the way he probably would have chosen!

Questions to Ponder

1. Growing up we all had dreams of one sort or the other. Do you feel like you are now where you always dreamed you'd be? Why or why not?

2. Remember, back when we studied Job we learned that Satan does not like when we are doing good and prospering in the kingdom of God. But what does Romans 8:31 say?

3. God had challenging words for Job in the end. But what was Job's reply in Job 42:2-3?

4. Since Joseph was a teenager when sold by his brothers, and then did not come to Pharaoh's palace until he was about thirty, that means he was in slavery or prison for thirteen years! But God's timing is different than ours. What does 2 Peter 3:8-9 say?

5. Joseph needed time to mature into who God wanted him to be, just like we often do. In Genesis 50:20-21, we see the pureness of Joseph's heart after his brothers come and beg for mercy. What does Joseph say, and how might this help you?

CHAPTER 6

RAISING BEAUTY FROM ASHES

To all who mourn … he will give a crown of beauty for ashes, a joyous blessing instead of mourning, festive praise instead of despair. In their righteousness, they will be like great oaks that the LORD has planted for his own glory.

Isaiah 61:3

BACK IN 2007, SALLIE SAXON was one of the most infamous inmates in North Carolina. Known as the "South Park Madam," she had been arrested for running what federal agents called the most successful prostitution ring in the country. It operated from some of Charlotte's swankiest hotels and served a client list that included prominent wealthy businessmen. Sallie's path in life included nearly thirty years of prostitution—eventually overseeing hundreds of prostituted women serving more than 2,000 clients.

But her life wasn't supposed to be like that.

Growing up Sallie lived most of the time with her grandparents, who provided a Christian environment. But Sallie was repeatedly devastated by her broken relationship with her mother and stepfather. During her visits with them, her stepfather would physically abuse her, sometimes while her mother watched. He also hurled insults at her and told her that she would become a prostitute someday.

One time her stepfather angrily beat Sallie with a belt after she became pregnant at age nineteen and refused his demand to get an abortion. She ended up spending three weeks in the hospital, barely avoiding a miscarriage.

She did marry the baby's father, but after also suffering physical abuse from him, they got divorced and Sallie struggled to make a living. Desperate for income, she agreed to a proposal from a wealthy businessman to entertain him and his associates.

But Sallie hated living that way—it was so humiliating.

"You feel so used. The men will literally throw their money on you and say, 'I paid for you. I bought you.'"

One afternoon she sat in her bathtub, ready to take more than two hundred Valium pills she had accumulated over the years.[12]

But guess what? That wasn't God's plan for Sallie! God redeemed her, and she then began visiting prisons, sharing her story to other women just like her. She did it to give them hope ...

I've already talked a bit about my childhood, but like Sallie Saxon, home-life while growing up wasn't always much fun. And things got a lot worse after my dad, who I loved dearly, disappeared forever from our lives when I was a young teen.

I felt abandoned by my dad, and didn't really feel loved by my mom—although in hindsight I know in her own way she did the best she could during those years. Regardless, during my teen years, I did a lot of "Looking for Love in All the Wrong Places," as the old country song goes.

But it never helped me feel better about myself. So I started drinking alcohol a lot, and experimented with different types of drugs to try and deaden the pain. Yet nothing ever really helped. Real change didn't come into my life until I came to know who Jesus was when I was in my mid-30s, after losing our two-year old son.

A couple years prior to completing this book, I started volunteering at camps for foster children. And at times I have overheard the kids talking of the abuse they are suffering at the hands of their parents, step-parents, or foster parents. Some have been thrown against walls, some have been beaten severely, and some have had to watch other family members being pulverized with shovels—as well as other items—to within an inch of their lives.

It breaks my heart. What will happen to these kids if they have to stay in these types of homes? How long will it take before they end up reaching out for other ways to deaden their pain like Sallie and I did?

It's difficult, because sometimes you feel so helpless. However, if there's nothing else you can do, you can always pray—so I do. I pray that somehow God will send into their lives godly influences that will teach them about Jesus, and teach them there is always hope. I pray they will learn they never need to feel afraid ever again.

There are three women in the Bible who really stand out to me. Why? Because, like Sallie Saxon, they also found themselves in situations that had to have been extremely humiliating, but God came alongside them in their embarrassment and struggles and brought them fresh starts and new lives.

Woman Caught in Adultery

In John 8:1-11, we come to a lady whose name we will not know until we meet her in heaven.

This account opens up with Jesus on the Mount of Olives teaching those who are following Him. Suddenly the self-righteous Pharisees bring to Him a woman, whom they throw down in front of Him: "'Teacher,' they said to Jesus, 'this woman was caught in the act of adultery. The law of Moses says to stone her. What do you say?'" [vv. 4-5]

However, the first part of verse six gives us the real reason they have brought her before Jesus: "They were trying to trap him into saying something they could use against him..." They wanted to trick Jesus, hoping to discredit Him and all that He had been doing. They hated Jesus because He was taking away their power and authority over the people. They were green with envy, wanting Him destroyed (Mark 2:1-3:6).

But back to the woman. After the Pharisees brought her to Jesus and made their claims, Jesus did something astounding. Rather than confront the issue immediately, "Jesus stooped down and wrote in the dust with his finger" (v. 6b).

There's been a lot of speculation about just what He was writing, but that's not the issue here. The issue is that the Pharisees kept hounding Jesus, so finally He straightens up, looks at them, and tells them: "'All right, but let the one who has never sinned throw the first stone!' Then he stooped down again and wrote in the dust" (vv. 7-8).

Clearly there's something supernatural going on, because it states in verses 9-11:

> When the accusers heard this, they slipped away one by one, beginning with the oldest, until only Jesus was left in the middle of the crowd with the woman. Then Jesus stood up again and said to the woman, 'Where are your accusers? Didn't even one of them condemn you?'
>
> 'No, Lord,' she said.
>
> And Jesus said, 'Neither do I. Go and sin no more.'

I often wonder about the underlying story of this unnamed woman. Was she a prostitute, or had she really been in love with the man?

And speaking of that man, where *was* he during all this, by the way? Did he come with the throng of Pharisees to throw her before Jesus—had it all been a wicked plot?

Was the woman set up from the beginning? Did her lover arrange with the Pharisees the time that he was to be with her? Were they watching the act through a window? Scripture doesn't tell us.

Think about her feelings of humiliation. She had been dragged in front of Jesus and a crowd of people by a group of men. How she felt meant absolutely nothing to them. They just wanted revenge, and she was a part of their plan.

How different it must have seemed after all the men left and she was left alone with Jesus! He didn't call her a harlot; He treated her with respect. But he did warn her how necessary it was to turn from her life of sin (v. 11), and that's something we all must remember.

Oh, the mercy and love of our Savior!

Rahab

The next woman we're going to study briefly, the Bible doesn't hesitate to call a prostitute or harlot. Her name? Rahab.

First, a little background.

After leading the Israelites for forty years, Moses dies and enters his Heavenly Home. Joshua is named as his successor (Deuteronomy 31:1-8), and is given the task of finally bringing the wandering Israelites into the Promised Land to start their new lives of freedom.

As we get to the book of Joshua, we see in chapter one that God promises to guide and direct Joshua, just like he did with Moses. So Joshua tells his officials to start getting the people ready to go.

Since the Promised Land was still occupied by their enemy the Canaanites, chapter two opens up with Joshua sending two spies over into the Promised Land to check it out, and they end up going to "the house of a prostitute named Rahab and stayed there that night" (v. 1). Rahab probably was the innkeeper of that house.

But the king of Jericho hears about the two spies who had come to her inn, and Rahab is ordered to turn them over to the king's authorities (vv. 2-3).

Here's where it gets really interesting:

> Rahab had hidden the two men, but she replied, 'Yes, the men were here earlier, but I didn't know where they were from. They left the town at dusk, as the gates were about to close. I don't know where they went. If you hurry, you can probably catch up with them.' (Actually she had taken them up to the roof and hidden them beneath bundles of flax she had laid out.) So the king's men went looking for the spies along the road leading to the shallow crossings of the Jordan River. And as soon as the king's men had left, the gate of Jericho was shut. [vv. 4-7]

Rahab lied to the king's officials! But why?

Our awesome God, that's why. He was working in her heart:

> Before the spies went to sleep that night, Rahab went up on the roof to talk with them. 'I know the LORD has given you this land,' she told them. 'We are all afraid of you. Everyone in the land is living in terror. For we have heard how the LORD made a dry path for you through the Red Sea when you left Egypt. And we know what you did to Sihon and Og, the two Amorite kings east of the Jordan River, whose people you completely

destroyed. No wonder our hearts have melted in fear! No one has the courage to fight after hearing such things. For the LORD your God is the supreme God of the heavens above and the earth below.

'Now swear to me by the LORD that you will be kind to me and my family since I have helped you. Give me some guarantee that when Jericho is conquered, you will let me live, along with my father and mother, my brothers and sisters, and all their families.' [vv. 8-13]

The two men agree as long as she doesn't tell the king's men, so Rahab lets them down by a rope through her window. That worked out well, because her house was situated on the city wall. She then gave the men instructions about where to hide, and told them to remain there in hiding for three days (vv. 14-20).

The spies trusted her, and did everything she told them to do.

We next hear of Rahab in chapter six. The Israelites are now following God's instructions to march around the city of Jericho for six days, and then on the seventh day they are to march around it seven times, with the trumpets sounding. The city wall collapses, allowing the Israelites to march in and overtake the city.

Amidst all the hoopla surrounding the supernatural collapse of the city walls, it would have been easy for them all to forget the promise they had made to Rahab. But remember, friends, God never forgets those He has chosen:

Meanwhile, Joshua said to the two spies, 'Keep your promise. Go to the prostitute's house and bring her out, along with all her family.'

The men who had been spies went in and brought out Rahab, her father, mother, brothers, and all the other relatives who were with her. They moved her whole family to a safe place near the camp of Israel.

Then the Israelites burned the town and everything in it. Only the things made from silver, gold, bronze, or iron were kept for the treasury of the LORD's house. So Joshua spared Rahab the prostitute and her relatives who were with her in the house, because she had hidden the spies Joshua sent to Jericho. And she lives among the Israelites to this day. [vv. 22-25]

Now ending Rahab's story would have been great right there, but something even more exciting happens to the dear woman. Look at Matthew 1:1-5:

This is a record of the ancestors of Jesus the Messiah, a descendant of David and of Abraham:

Abraham was the father of Isaac. Isaac was the father of Jacob. Jacob was the father of Judah and his brothers.

Judah was the father of Perez and Zerah (whose mother was Tamar). Perez the father of Hezron. Hezron was the father of Ram.

Ram was the father of Amminadab. Amminadab was the father of Nahshon. Nahshon the father of Salmon.

Salmon was the father of Boaz, (*whose mother was Rahab*)... [emphasis mine]

Did you see that? Rahab is listed in the genealogy of Jesus!

Never underestimate what God wants to do with your life. It doesn't matter where you have been, or where you are now. Our Heavenly Father knows your heart—deep down inside you—and He knows all the hurts you've experienced. Don't give up; trust Him to do the impossible with you, just as He did with Rahab.

The Samaritan Woman

The story of the last woman I want to touch on as we conclude this chapter is in John 4:1-42. This is the story of a Samaritan woman, and how Jesus turned this woman shunned by society into a great witness for God Himself.

Again, first a little background.

The Samaritans were shunned by the Jewish people because after the Assyrian captivity of northern Israel around 721 BC, many who stayed behind intermarried with the Assyrians, which they were told not to do. They then built their own temple, put together their own copy of the Torah (first five books of the Old Testament), and also had their own religion which combined Judaism with paganism. For this reason the Jewish people called them unclean.

As we start off reading this chapter, we see that Jesus has decided to travel through Samaria, which was typically avoided by the Jewish people. So why did He decide to go *through* Samaria instead of around? Because He knew there was a woman who needed Him there.

It is the heat of the day, and Jesus in His human body is tired and thirsty after the journey. He stops at Jacob's well in Samaria and sits down to rest.

Normally people would come to gather water from the well in the evenings when it was cooler, but here in the middle of the day suddenly a woman approaches. Jesus knows this woman is coming to draw water at this particular time to avoid the sneers and jeers of her fellow countrymen.

When she arrives at the well, Jesus looks at her and asks if she will draw him a drink of water.

She can tell that Jesus is not a Samaritan, so she asks Him why He came. Why in the world was He asking her for water? Samaritans and Jews did not associate with each other!

Jesus tells her:

'If you only knew the gift God has for you and who you are speaking to, you would ask me, and I would give you living water …

'Anyone who drinks this water will soon become thirsty again. But those who drink the water I give will never be thirsty again. It becomes a fresh, bubbling spring within them, giving them eternal life.' [vv. 10, 13-14]

In v. 15 we see that the woman is drawn to Him by His words—no doubt about it: '"Please, sir," the woman said, "give me this water! Then I'll never be thirsty again, and I won't have to come here to get water."'

But Jesus wanted her to fully understand just who He was and what He was really saying:

'Go and get your husband,' Jesus told her.

'I don't have a husband,' the woman replied.

Jesus said, 'You're right! You don't have a husband—
for you have had five husbands, and you aren't even
married to the man you're living with now. You certainly
spoke the truth!'

'Sir,' the woman said, 'you must be a prophet. So tell me,
why is it that you Jews insist that Jerusalem is the only
place of worship, while we Samaritans claim it is here
at Mount Gerizim, where our ancestors worshiped?'

Jesus replied, 'Believe me, dear woman, the time is
coming when it will no longer matter whether you
worship the Father on this mountain or in Jerusalem.
You Samaritans know very little about the one you
worship, while we Jews know all about him, for
salvation comes through the Jews. But the time is
coming—indeed it's here now—when true worshipers
will worship the Father in spirit and in truth. The Father
is looking for those who will worship him that way. For
God is Spirit, so those who worship him must worship
in spirit and in truth.'

The woman said, 'I know that Messiah is coming—
the one who is called Christ. When he comes, he will
explain everything to us.'

Then Jesus told her, 'I AM the Messiah!' [vv. 16-26]

Wow, what a conversation! I can't even imagine what that must
have been like.

It is hard in our human minds to fully comprehend the working
ways of the Holy Spirit, but Scripture is clear that through this
Samaritan woman's conversation with Jesus, she suddenly believes
that Jesus is who He says He is. And she is so excited after hearing

His words that she forgets all about her water jar and runs back into town telling people right and left that she has encountered who she believes is Jesus Christ, the Messiah (vv. 28-29).

So how does this story end? Numerous Samaritans turn to true faith in Jesus because of the testimony of a woman they had previously shunned (v. 42). She is no longer an outcast!

Questions to Ponder

1. Have you ever been in a situation like the woman caught in adultery where suddenly you found yourself completely exposed in your shame? What did you do?

2. Do you sometimes feel like you've made too many mistakes in your life for God to forgive you? If so, why do you feel that way?

3. Isaiah 42:1-9 is a prophecy about Jesus. How does v. 3 say He will treat us?

4. King David was a man after God's own heart (Acts 13:22). Yet one day he sins horribly by sleeping with Bathsheba, and then sends her husband to his death (2 Samuel 11 and 12)! God sends His prophet Nathan to talk to him, and David tearfully repents. Shortly after, David writes Psalm 51. What does he admit in Psalm 51:4?

5. We all mess-up and fall short of how we should live at times (Romans 3:23). However, what promise do we have according to 1 John 2:1?

CHAPTER 7

GET BETTER, NOT BITTER

Blessed (happy, to be envied) is the man who is patient under trial and stands up under temptation, for when he has stood the test and been approved, he will receive [the victor's] crown of life which God has promised to those who love Him.

James 1:12 AMP

ON A SEPTEMBER MORNING IN 2001, Frank Silecchia laced up his boots, put on his hardhat, and headed out the door of his New Jersey house. As a construction worker, his job was to make things. But as a volunteer at the World Trade Center wreckage, he was having a very hard time making sense of it all. He had hoped to find live bodies. He did not. Instead, he found dead ones.

Frank had just pulled three lifeless bodies from beneath the rubble when he saw amid the destruction a heavenly symbol—a twenty-foot tall steel-beam cross. No winch had hoisted it, no cement secured it. The iron beams were standing independent of human help. Exhausted and traumatized by his labors, the man dropped to his knees in tears.

"It was a sign," Frank recalled later, "a sign that God hadn't deserted us."[13]

It was said the beams of the large cross had been melted together from the intense heat. They were two girders which had been bonded into one, forged by the fire.[14]

God sent a symbol amidst the destruction. A cross in the crisis. We can ask, "Where has God been while all this has been happening to me?" The answer: "Right in the middle of it all, walking right beside us."

On December 25, 2015 the weather where we were living in Texas was hovering around the 80 degree mark. We were loving it.

The next day? Approximately twelve tornadoes swirled all around our area, killing thirteen people, and completely destroying numerous homes. Christmases were lost and forgotten as families struggled to survive. We were thankful that our house was not hit and suffered no damage.

Realistically, every single one of us have been through times of severe pain and sorrow to some degree or the other, haven't we?

But it is hard to remember that we are not the only ones suffering when we're facing heartbreak, grief, and pain. Because when we are right smack dab in the middle of our trials we hurt, sometimes so badly that we feel we can't even breathe.

You may feel like you are totally alone, and sometimes you may find you are having trouble even getting out of bed. It is too hard. You just want to sleep, because maybe if you sleep longer you'll find it has all just been a bad dream.

But sleep doesn't come.

So you lay there in bed, and then the questions start popping into your head at a frantic pace: *Why does no one seem to care? Why does no one come and tell me that everything is going to be okay?*

That's where hope comes in. Without hope we have nothing. And if we don't have God in our lives, we really cannot have hope. We need to cling to God, choosing to trust Him even when it seems as though we may never stop hurting again.

Romans 15:13 (NIV) says, "May the God of *hope* fill you with all joy and peace as you trust in him, so that you may overflow with *hope* by the power of the Holy Spirit" (emphasis mine).

Real Hope is a totally supernatural thing.

When you have Real Hope, you find it's totally different than "hoping" the job promotion will come through, or "hoping" that the cute guy in class will ask you out.

Real Hope stands firm and brings you through whatever trial you are facing, giving you ultimate victory.

One day, not too long after losing our two-year old son, I was having a major melt-down in our bedroom. I was lying curled up like a ball on the floor in front of our bed, crying my eyes out.

"Lord, we're never going to be able to take Matthew to Disneyland!"

It was then that I heard God's still small voice softly saying to me, "Do you not think where he is right now is better than Disneyland?"

Of course it was!

Then I saw a vision in my head of our little boy Matthew walking on the clouds, holding tightly to Jesus's hand. He was looking up and smiling at Jesus's face, and Jesus was smiling back at him. He looked so happy! Matthew was even wearing his favorite Atlanta Braves baseball cap that his uncle had given him.

I continued to lay on my bedroom floor after that, still crying. But this time my tears were different. This time my tears were thankful tears, because I knew without a doubt that Matthew was being taken care of so much better than we could have ever taken care of him. Plus, I was filled with joy knowing I was going to be able to see all my kids again, in a place where there will be no more tears, sorrow, or pain (Revelation 21:4).

One of my favorite people in the Bible is the Apostle Peter. Why? Because he is just so human!

When Peter was called by Jesus to follow Him, he was a simple fisherman. He was a man who worked hard in the trade industry for many hours a day in all types of weather.

What do you think of when you think of a fisherman? I am thinking he had to have been strong physically in order to haul in the heavy nets of fish (no fancy-rigged fishing boats back then), and his skin was most likely sunburnt and weathered from working outside for hours on end. Rugged-looking is a word that comes to my mind.

Acts 4:13 tells us that he was unschooled—he was just an ordinary guy.

You also find as you read through the Gospels that he was brash sometimes, strong-willed, and impulsive. Yet he became one of the first followers of Jesus. I love that!

His birth name was Simon, but when Jesus laid His eyes on him, he changed his name to Cephas (Aramaic), or Peter (Greek), which means "rock" (John 1:42).

The day that Peter confesses his belief in Jesus as the Son of God, look at what happens:

> Jesus replied, 'You are blessed, Simon son of John, because my Father in heaven has revealed this to you. You did not learn this from any human being. Now I say to you that you are Peter (which means 'rock'), and upon this rock I will build my church, and all the powers of hell will not conquer it. And I will give you the keys of the Kingdom of Heaven. Whatever you forbid on earth will be forbidden in heaven, and whatever you permit on earth will be permitted in heaven.' [Matthew 16:17-19]

Pretty heavy news for a fisherman to hear, huh?

Peter went on to show himself as a natural-born leader by becoming the main mouth-piece of the disciples (Matthew 15:15, 19:27).

He also was a part of the inner circle of the disciples, along with James and John. Only those three were present when Jesus raised the daughter of Jairus from the dead (Mark 5:37), and when Jesus was transfigured on the mountain (Matthew 17:1).

Yet through all that, Peter remained ... well ... Peter. Even after walking side-by-side with Jesus for three years, Peter still struggled with "humanness," just like we all do.

In so many instances, the rash and impetuous side of Peter rose to the surface, such as in Matthew 14:25-31, when the disciples are by themselves out in the middle of the Sea of Galilee:

> About three o'clock in the morning Jesus came toward them, walking on the water. When the disciples saw him walking on the water, they were terrified. In their fear, they cried out, 'It's a ghost!'
>
> But Jesus spoke to them at once. 'Don't be afraid,' he said. 'Take courage. I am here!'
>
> Then Peter called to him, 'Lord, if it's really you, tell me to come to you, walking on the water.'
>
> 'Yes, come,' Jesus said.
>
> So Peter went over the side of the boat and walked on the water toward Jesus. But when he saw the strong wind and the waves, he was terrified and began to sink. 'Save me, Lord!' he shouted.
>
> Jesus immediately reached out and grabbed him. 'You have so little faith,' Jesus said. 'Why did you doubt me?'

Have you ever taken a giant leap into something and then realized you were in over your head? I have!

Then came the time of Jesus's betrayal by one of the original disciples, Judas. Judas had with him a guard of soldiers, as well as the chief priests and Pharisees who had been opposed to Jesus and His teachings. Jesus had been usurping their authority, and they hadn't liked it one bit! So they came to arrest Him.

Peter certainly didn't like seeing that. John 18:10-11 tells us: "Then Simon Peter drew a sword and slashed off the right ear of Malchus, the high priest's slave. But Jesus said to Peter, 'Put your sword back into its sheath. Shall I not drink from the cup of suffering the Father has given me?'"

Ouch! I have to say I really can't blame Peter, as he didn't fully understand all of what was going on and acted on impulse. He was trying to protect Jesus, forgetting that Jesus really didn't need protecting ...

However, Peter's greatest point of grief came when he got a little cocky after the Lord's last supper:

> ... Jesus told [the disciples], 'Tonight all of you will desert me. For the Scriptures say, 'God will strike the Shepherd, and the sheep will be scattered.' But after I have been raised from the dead, I will go ahead of you to Galilee and meet you there.'
>
> Peter declared, 'Even if everyone else deserts you, I will never desert you.'
>
> Jesus replied, 'I tell you the truth, Peter—this very night, before the rooster crows, you will deny three times that you even know me.'
>
> 'No!' Peter insisted. 'Even if I have to die with you, I will never deny you.' [Matthew 26:31-35]

You probably know the story: Unfortunately Peter did just what he had promised Jesus he would never do.

After Jesus was arrested, Peter bravely followed Him and the arresting soldiers all the way to the courtyard of the high priest. Then he sat down to wait and see how everything was going to play out:

> Meanwhile, Peter was sitting outside in the courtyard. A servant girl came over and said to him, 'You were one of those with Jesus the Galilean.'
>
> But Peter denied it in front of everyone. 'I don't know what you're talking about,' he said.
>
> Later, out by the gate, another servant girl noticed him and said to those standing around, 'This man was with Jesus of Nazareth.'
>
> Again Peter denied it, this time with an oath. 'I don't even know the man,' he said.
>
> A little later some of the other bystanders came over to Peter and said, 'You must be one of them; we can tell by your Galilean accent.'
>
> Peter swore, 'A curse on me if I'm lying—I don't know the man!' And immediately the rooster crowed.
>
> Suddenly Jesus' words flashed through Peter's mind: 'Before the rooster crows, you will deny three times that you even know me.' And he went away, weeping bitterly. [Matthew 26:69-75]

My heart breaks when I think of how horribly Peter must have felt.

There have been many times when I've found myself somewhat in Peter's shoes and have denied Jesus, as well. Maybe I haven't deliberately told people I'm not a Christian, but I have certainly turned away from witnessing to somebody who doesn't yet know Him, laughed at inappropriate jokes, or pretended that I didn't see any problem with a sin a friend is committing right before my eyes.

We have all had those moments, haven't we?

But getting back to Peter—remember Jesus's promise that Peter would be the rock upon which the church was built (Matthew 16:17-19)? Well when God promises something, you can be sure that He will keep it, no matter how deep a pit we dig for ourselves.

One day after Jesus's resurrection from the dead, we find Peter and some of the other disciples on the shores of the Sea of Galilee. Peter suddenly decides he's going fishing.

Why did Peter suddenly decide to do that? What had been going through his mind right then? Did he just need to occupy his mind by doing something he knew how to do well, and that he did not need to think much about?

Of course we cannot know for sure. But for me, when I'm getting down on myself about how I have really messed something up, I try and turn my mind to something where I don't have to think, period!

Who knows? Maybe Peter had been standing on the shore that day feeling shackled with guilt as he remembered how he failed Jesus. Maybe he was remembering all the times when he and Jesus had walked side-by-side, eating and sharing life together. Scripture doesn't say.

Let's pick back up with Peter's story in John 21:3-9:

> Simon Peter said [to the disciples with him], 'I'm going fishing.'
>
> 'We'll come too,' they all said. So they went out in the boat, but they caught nothing all night.
>
> At dawn Jesus was standing on the beach, but the disciples couldn't see who he was. He called out, 'Fellows, have you caught any fish?'
>
> 'No,' they replied.
>
> Then he said, 'Throw out your net on the right-hand side of the boat, and you'll get some!' So they did, and they couldn't haul in the net because there were so many fish in it.
>
> Then the disciple Jesus loved said to Peter, 'It's the Lord!' When Simon Peter heard that it was the Lord, he put on his tunic (for he stripped for work), jumped into the water, and headed to shore. The others stayed with the boat and pulled the loaded net to the shore, for they were only about a hundred yards from shore. When they got there, they found breakfast waiting for them—fish cooking over a charcoal fire, and some bread.

Jesus is there waiting for them, and has cooked them breakfast! Always thinking of others first, in love.

As you continue reading John 21, you see that Jesus sits and talks to Peter after breakfast, reminding him that He has chosen Peter to preach and teach the Gospel.

What happens next? Incredible stuff! Not long after that, Peter ends up preaching to a huge crowd of people on the day of Pentecost where approximately 3,000 people become new believers (Acts 2:42). Later he heals a lame man (Acts 3:6-8), speaks boldly to the Sanhedrin council who had opposed Jesus so bitterly (Acts 4:1-4), and even through imprisonment and floggings refuses to ever deny his beliefs again because of everything Jesus had done for him (Acts 5:17-42).

On top of that, God used Peter to write the books of 1 and 2 Peter in the Bible, full of richness about God's righteousness and holiness, as well as a great guidebook on how we are supposed to be living—even when we suffer!

Peter had, indeed, become the rock of the church that Jesus said he would be.

Did that mean he never messed up again? Absolutely not! He still struggled at times with what God was asking him to do, just like us (see Acts 10:9-14, Galatians 2:11-13).

Questions to Ponder

1. Can you think of a time when you'd lost hope in something, and then suddenly you witnessed God coming through in a miraculous way?

2. When things are going bad, we need to get our focus back to the One who is with us always. What does Deuteronomy 31:6 say?

3. What is the great promise Matthew 11:28-30 has for us?

4. Do you believe that God will use you through your trials—faults and all—just as He used Peter? Why or why not?

5. We all make mistakes, and that's one of the many reasons I love to read about Peter. However, like Peter, when we make bad choices God will sift and churn us until we get back to where He wants us to be. What is the promise stated in 1 Peter 5:10?

CHAPTER 8

IN A NUTSHELL

Finally, let no one cause me trouble, for
I bear on my body the marks of Jesus.
Galatians 6:17 NIV

A WHILE BACK I READ a short story about a man and his young daughter. The man's name was Richard Cecil. One day his little girl was sitting on his knee, and she held in her hands her favorite pretty glass-bead necklace. Richard asked his daughter if she truly loved him, and, if so, did she love him enough to take her pretty beads and toss them into the burning fireplace?

His little girl stared at her daddy's face—she couldn't believe that he would ask such a thing from her! But his steady gaze convinced her that he was being completely serious. So with trembling reluctant steps she tottered to the fire grate and dropped the beads into the fire. She then flung herself into her daddy's arms, crying until she had no more tears to cry. She was heartbroken from her loss.

A few days later was her birthday, and on that day she discovered laying on her dresser a little package. She opened it and found inside a cluster of *real* pearls strung upon a necklace. It had her name on it, and was signed with love from her father. She flew to his presence, threw herself in his arms and said, "Oh, Papa, I am so sorry that I did not understand."[15]

Precious readers, someday we too will understand. We will understand why we have had to experience the pain and grief that we have gone through.

Take a look at Galatians 6:17 at the start of this chapter again. The word "marks" means "brand." We, as God's children, bear the brand of being a part of God's family. Sometimes our marks may not seem visible to others at first, but as people get to know us our brand will begin to glow bright and clear to the watching world, demonstrating that we are children of the King.

This is what the Apostle Paul was talking about when he wrote about his marks to the Galatian church. Many people during that time did not believe he was a true Apostle because he did not hold to the ceremonial practices taught in that day. But here Paul is saying, in effect, "It doesn't matter what you say or how you think of me—take a good look at my life and witness what I've gone through!"

As you studied previously in chapter three of this book, Paul suffered illnesses, imprisonments, and severe beatings all for his love and devotion to Jesus.

At times we all must endure the sharpness of the brand of Jesus's cross. Sometimes it seems as if our pain and suffering are never going to end. But someday—yes, someday—everything will make sense and we will be so thankful that we ourselves were able to bear the marks of Jesus as we sit at His feet in our heavenly home, never to be hurt again.

To end, we've barely scratched the surface of a few great heroes of the Bible, and how their trials shaped them. But one day we will be able to meet them all, *provided* we have made Jesus our Lord, and have relinquished our lives to Him, believing that He died on the cross for us and rose again.

Let's briefly recap what we've studied:

In **chapter one,** we learned about Grace Gonzalez, and how she carried self-proclaimed blame for her sister's death into years of alcohol and drug abuse before she got to the point of trying to end her life. She then learned in a miraculous way that God was real, and that He loved her so very much.

We also looked at the prophet Jonah, and how his preconceived idea of how things should be in life almost caused a whole shipload of sailors to drown at sea. Then he got upset when God saved a city full of people—because Jonah felt they didn't deserve it.

In **chapter two,** we learned about Joni Eareckson Tada whose life took a drastic turn when a diving accident as a teenager turned her into a quadriplegic, placing her full-time in a wheelchair. She remains faithful, not understanding fully why God allowed all that to happen, yet trusting that He will take care of her.

We also learned about the prophet Jeremiah, who obeyed God's call on his life (after making numerous excuses), and then was told he would suffer greatly as he spoke to the nations. The questions, pain, and grief he lived with are beyond our imagination. Yet he also remained faithful in all that God asked him to do.

In **chapter three**, we heard about Karla Faye Tucker, who was sentenced to death for murder. She and her boyfriend hadn't planned to kill anyone, but they were high on drugs and things got out of control. Yet through this horrible crime, God used her imprisonment to teach her what was really important.

We also read about the Apostle Paul. He was arrogant and boastful. He had been trained by the best teachers in the church, and he would do whatever was necessary to keep doing what he thought was right—even killing innocent people! However, God always has a way of getting our attention, and one day on the road to Damascus Paul was brought to his knees by the Truth.

In **chapter four**, we learned that sometimes God might allow the things we hold dearest to be taken away from us. Amy Carmichael had been serving young girls who had been forced into prostitution for over thirty years as a missionary when she was struck with a debilitating illness that forced her to be bedridden for the remainder of her life.

We also talked about Job, a man who treated people fairly and did all he could to take care of his family. He would offer sacrifices for his children "just in case" they had sinned. Yet suddenly things took a turn for the worse when he ended up losing everything he owned, and then was covered with painful sores all over his body. To top it off, the "friends" who came to offer him support ended up causing him more pain than help. Yet God fully redeemed Job in the end, prospering him with more than he had before.

In **chapter five,** we touched upon John McCain who was serving his country in the military when suddenly he was shot down by enemy fire and kept in various Vietnamese prison camps for over five years. He was repeatedly tortured and severely beaten. Yet through those years God sent him little signs that he was right there with him—he was not forgotten.

We also studied about Joseph. Since he was his father's favorite son, his brothers despised him, throwing him into a pit and selling him into slavery. His life for years after was like a recurring bad dream. He kept doing the best he could, yet kept getting burned by people he trusted. But we learned that God never wastes the trials we go through. He uses our pain and suffering to mold and shape us into individuals who have the potential to reach thousands of people to change their lives.

In **chapter six,** we came upon Sallie Saxon, who, because of the abuse she suffered in her late teens, suddenly found herself embroiled in a world of prostitution and high-class call girls. She became famous, but the fame she had acquired was not the kind she was proud of. Yet Jesus rescued Sallie, and now she is a beautiful, confident woman helping others that have found themselves in situations such as her own.

We also touched upon three women in the Bible that you might call unsavory—just like Sallie used to think of herself. They were the woman caught in adultery, Rahab, and the Samaritan woman.

These women were also shunned by society, yet their stories show that God's love reaches across all boundaries. No matter what we have done, or where we have been, God can and will use us to shine His light to a dark and dying world.

In **chapter seven,** we learned about Frank Silecchia, a common person like most of us. Then came the day he found himself volunteering to sift through the rubble after 9/11, where he came upon devastation and despair few of us will ever see. Yet just when he was feeling like God had truly deserted him, he came upon a "cross in the crisis," which made him realize that God had His eyes on him and had not forgotten him.

We also read about the Apostle Peter, a common fisherman, who became one of the original twelve disciples of Jesus. But one day he made a promise he did not keep to Jesus, and it destroyed him inwardly. Yet like Frank Silecchia, God pulled Peter out of the muck and mire that had filled his mind, and Peter ended up being one of the central mouthpieces for spreading the Gospel. Talk about exciting!

In closing up this chapter, I just want to spur you on to keep your eyes on Jesus, no matter how hard it seems sometimes. Yes, at times it will be extremely difficult, but He will be there to help you, even when you're at your lowest and just can't seem to keep your head up.

And you know what? I firmly believe in my heart that one day, once we are safe in our heavenly home with Jesus, people will be coming up to *you*, saying, "Thank you … thank you for helping me when I needed it the most."

CHAPTER 9

FINAL THOUGHTS

Jesus said to him, You do not understand now what I am doing, but you will understand later on. (John 13:7 AMP)

As a recap, here are just some of the reasons God allows us to go through trials:

- Conforms us to His image
- Gives us power to witness
- Instills in us God-sufficiency
- Catches the attention of the watching world
- Enables us to help others through similar trials
- Teaches us perseverance, humility, patience, and love
- Focuses our eyes on eternity
- Molds and refines us
- Strengthens our faith

Now, I don't doubt the above list is incomplete. Yet I know whatever the reason, God will use what you have gone through—if you let Him. And I know that with complete certainty!

My friends, remember that you are precious and so special in God's sight. Nothing, and I mean *nothing* that you have done is so terrible that you cannot run to God and ask Him to save you. He has great plans for *you,* just as He has for me.

My prayer is that you who have read this short book will feel closer to God than ever before.

In no way am I an extraordinary individual—I am a regular person just like you. Yet I have chosen to place the Lord Jesus first and foremost in my life, trusting that whatever He has in store for me will be just the right thing. He can and will do the same thing for you, *provided* that you choose to have a personal relationship with Him, making Him *your* Lord, as well.

So many people (believe me, I was one of them) think that all their freedom will be gone if they turn their lives over to Jesus. Before losing our boys, I felt I was fully capable of handling my life all by myself. I figured as long as I was a pretty good person God would have mercy on me when I died, and I would immediately go up into heaven.

I was blinded, just like many of you are, by the deceit in this world and by the enemy of our souls who is trying to sway people away from God. The truth of the matter is that I feel freer now in my life than I ever felt before! I need never worry, because I know that my Heavenly Father is looking out for me every minute of every day. He has *promised* to care for all my needs, just as He will for yours.

In Matthew 6:26-33, Jesus tells us:

Look at the birds. They don't plant or harvest or store food in barns, for your heavenly Father feeds them. And aren't you far more valuable to him than they are? Can all your worries add a single moment to your life?

And why worry about your clothing? Look at the lilies of the field and how they grow. They don't work or make their clothing, yet Solomon in all his glory was not dressed as beautifully as they are. And if God cares so wonderfully for wildflowers that are here today and thrown into the fire tomorrow, he will certainly care for you. Why do you have so little faith?

So don't worry about these things, saying, 'What will we eat? What will we drink? What will we wear?' These things dominate the thoughts of unbelievers, but your heavenly Father already knows all your needs. Seek the Kingdom of God above all else, and live righteously, and he will give you everything you need.

When the Pharisees asked Jesus what the most important commandment was, He replied: "'You must love the LORD your God with all your heart, all your soul, and all your mind.' This is the first and greatest commandment. A second is equally important: 'Love your neighbor as yourself'" (Matthew 22:37–39). That is really not too difficult, is it? If we are loving Jesus and are putting Him first—and if we are loving our neighbors as well—He will do wonderful and amazing things in our lives.

So, how can you obtain this wonderful personal relationship with Jesus? Very simply. You just need to pray a prayer such as this one:

Dear Lord Jesus, I know that I am a sinner, and I ask You for Your forgiveness. I believe You died for my sins and rose from the dead. I turn from my sins and invite You to come into my heart and life. I want to trust and follow You as my Lord. In Your name I pray. Amen.

In closing, I pray that all who read this book may experience the true love, grace, and peace of our Lord Jesus Christ. He is waiting for you to come to Him, no matter where you find yourself at the moment. He is capable of reaching out to you *wherever* you are.

May God richly bless each and every one of you.

ENDNOTES

Chapter 1

1   The 700 Club, Releasing the Painful Memories of Childhood, http://
    www1.cbn.com/video/SAL112v2/releasing-the-painful-memories-of-
    childhood#Guest Info

2   Linda Kennedy, *The God of All Comfort*, Westbow Press, 2015

Chapter 2

3   CBN News, 50 Years Later--Joni Eareckson Tada Talks of On-Going
    Struggles, www1.cbn.com/cbnnews/us/2016/november/50-years-
    later-joni-eareckson-tada-talks-of-on-going-struggles

Chapter 3

4   CNN.com, Larry King, Karla Faye Tucker: Born again on death row,
    www.cnn.com/2007/US/03/21/larry.king.tucker

5   Significance of the Apostle Paul, 2003-2018 W.J. Rayment, www.
    biblestudyinfo.com/paul/biography.shtml

Chapter 4

6   Christianity.com, Amy Carmichael Helped the Helpless, July 16, 2010,
    www.christianity.com/church/church-history/church-history-for-kids/
    amy-carmichael-helped-the-helpless-11634859.html

7   Dohnavur Fellowship, Children's Home and Community in South
    India, continues the work that Amy Carmichael began in 1901,
    Dohnavur Fellowship 2013, www.dohnavurfellowship.org.in

8   Inspirational Christians, Amy Carmichael Biography, Haley Bradfield,
    www.inspirationalchristians.org/biography/amy-carmichael-
    biography

Chapter 5

9   History Channel, John McCain, BIO.com, http://www.history.com/topics/john-mccain

10 beliefnet, "The Moment I came to Love My Enemy, http://www.beliefnet.com/inspiration/2005/12/the-moment-i-came-to-love-my-enemy.aspx

11 His Eye is on the Sparrow, Civilla D. Martin, 1905, 08/07/2007, http://cyberhymnal.org/htm/h/i/hiseyeis.htm

Chapter 6

12 Charles Chandler, "Can a Prostitute be Redeemed?" *Decision Magazine*, Billy Graham Evangelical Association, February 2015, 20-21

Chapter 7

13 Rick Hampson, USA TODAY, "Ground Zero cross a powerful symbol for 9/11 museum" May15, 2014, https://www.usatoday.com/story/news/nation/2014/05/13/911-ground-zero-museum-cross-world-trade-center/8907003/

14 TVCatholic, "The 9/11 Ground Zero Cross—Beams Melted Together To Form The Cross" September 11, 2011, https://www.youtube.com/watch?v=O8GHUGAaOpY

Chapter 8

15 Worthy Christian Library, "Chapter 3—The Brand of the Cross" http://www.worthychristianlibrary.com/ab-simpson/cross-of-christ/chapter-3-the-brand-of-the-cross/

ACKNOWLEDGMENTS

I thank my God every time I remember you.
Philippians 1:3 NIV

I OWE SO MANY PEOPLE gratitude for writing this book.

First off, my Lord Jesus—without Him I am nothing. I adore You, Lord.

My husband Gary has stood by me through all my "yo-yo" phases of life. I know at times it was difficult, but without you believing in me, I don't know where I'd be.

Our remaining son, Jeffrey. I love you so much; and I can't wait for the day when we can live close together again sharing laughter, movies and Cheetos.

Without the encouragement of my friends Laura and Shelia, this book might not ever have been written. Thanks for believing in me.

My prayer partner Cheryl who at times will just sit and listen as I once again start to question, "What am I doing?" I appreciate you always being straightforward with me, and getting me back in line when needed.

Charly, my new friend who kindly offered to proof this book (without me asking), and gave me her honest opinions. I'm wowed by your friendship.

And Benj, my new friend who has patiently stood by me, helping me through the editing, publishing, and formatting of this book. Thank you for all your insight!

Linda Kennedy learned from firsthand experience that no matter how dark and troubled life becomes, when you surrender to Jesus Christ, healing can come. Read her story in the book *The God of All Comfort*. You can also connect with her at www.thegodofallcomfort.com, or on Facebook: @GodAllComfort.

Available from your favorite bookseller:

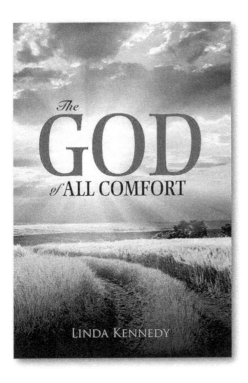

CPSIA information can be obtained
at www.ICGtesting.com
Printed in the USA
LVHW030024181121
703526LV00001B/66